BEYOND LANGUAGE

Cross-Cultural Communication

SECOND EDITION

Deena R. Levine, M.A.
Mara B. Adelman, Ph.D.

PRENTICE HALL REGENTS
Englewood Cliffs, New Jersey 07632

Library of Congress Cataloging-in-Publication Data

Levine, Deena R.
  Beyond language: cross-cultural communication / Deena R. Levine,
Mara B. Adelman.—2nd ed.
    p. cm.
  Includes bibliographical references.
  ISBN 0–13–094855–1
  1. English language—Textbooks for foreign speakers.
2. Intercultural communication. I. Adelman, Mara B. II. Title.
PE1128.L4597 1993   92–28675
428.2'4—dc20   CIP

Acquisitions editor: Nancy Leonhardt
Editorial/production supervision and
    interior design: Peggy M. Gordon
Copy editor: Sherry Babbitt
Cover design and interior illustrations: Hillel Levine
Photo research: Page Poore
Prepress buyer: Ray Keating
Manufacturing buyer: Lori Bulwin

Credits: *Pages 2, 9, 38, 173 (bottom):* Eugene Gordon. *Page 7:* AP/Wide World Photos. *Page 10:* United Nations. *Page 11:* Pan American Airways. *Pages 14, 43, 45, 67, 98, 102, 104, 106, 119–121, 136, 246, 250 (bottom), 256:* Irene Springer. *Page 34:* Minoru Aoki, Rapho/Photo Researchers. *Page 40:* Alexander Lowry/Photo Researchers. *Pages 62 (top), 105, 141, 144, 183, 204, 211, 212, 245 (bottom), 250 (top):* Laima Druskis. *Pages 66, 132, 138, 139, 180, 182, 215, 254:* Ken Karp. *Page 69 (left):* Al Giese/New York University. *Page 69 (right):* New York University Photographic Department. *Page 71:* Malcolm Anderson, U.S. Table Tennis Association. *Page 107:* Marc Anderson. *Page 142:* Shirley Zeiberg. *Page 169:* Charles Gatewood. *Page 173 (top):* United Nations/Bruno J. Zehnder. *Page 175:* Page Poore. *Pages 209, 257, 258:* A.T.&T. Co. Photo Center. *Page 214:* John Pitkin. *Page 216:* Courtesy of University of Kentucky Information Services. *Page 240:* Teri Leigh Stratford. *Page 244:* Hakim Raquib. *Page 248:* Bob David.

©1993, 1982 by Prentice Hall Regents
Prentice-Hall, Inc.
A Paramount Communications Company
Englewood Cliffs, New Jersey 07632

Printed in the United States of America
10   9   8   7

ISBN 0-13-094855-1

Prentice-Hall International (UK) Limited, *London*
Prentice-Hall of Australia Pty. Limited, *Sydney*
Prentice-Hall Canada Inc., *Toronto*
Prentice-Hall Hispanoamericana, S.A., *Mexico*
Prentice-Hall of India Private Limited, *New Delhi*
Prentice-Hall of Japan, Inc., *Tokyo*
Simon & Schuster Asia Pte. Ltd., *Singapore*
Editora Prentice-Hall do Brasil, Ltda., *Rio de Janeiro*

I do not want my house to be walled in on all sides and my windows to be stuffed. I want the cultures of all lands to be blown about my house as freely as possible. But I refuse to be blown off my feet by any.

Mahatma Gandhi

Contents

7 Education: Values and Expectations　205

8 Work: Practices and Attitudes　241

Preface

"To know another's language and not his culture is a very good way to make a fluent fool of one's self."[1]

The English as a second or foreign language (ESL or EFL) classroom lends itself naturally to the integration of language and cross-cultural teaching. Yet in many ESL/EFL courses students receive only random exposure to aspects of culture that are necessary for successful cross-cultural communication. The cultural use of English as well as an understanding of cultural values and attitudes should be incorporated into language programs designed to teach language competence. To learn to function in another language one must become comfortable in the culture of the new language and in face-to-face communication.

Beyond Language: Cross-Cultural Communication uses the subject areas of U.S. culture and cross-cultural communication as a vehicle for teaching English. The information presented is intended to help students understand and adapt to American culture and to cultural differences affecting their communication with speakers of American English. The objectives of *Beyond Language: Cross-Cultural Communication* fall into two categories:

Language Objectives

1. To broaden reading and conversational vocabulary

ix

2. To develop reading skills

3. To increase conversational fluency

Cross-Cultural Objectives

1. To provide an understanding of mainstream American culture and to raise awareness of cultural diversity within the United States

2. To increase the student's knowledge of cultural conflict and adjustment

3. To explain specific American patterns of communication that can lead to misunderstandings

4. To describe patterns of communication and culture that contrast with American patterns

The textbook has been designed to permit a systematic and graded presentation of language and culture. Each chapter has two distinct sections: (1) readings and exercises about cross-cultural communication and selected areas of American culture, and (2) conversational activities designed to promote discussion of the subtleties of cross-cultural communication. The focus on values, behavior, attitudes, and communication styles in the chapter readings is designed to serve as background for the accompanying conversational activities. The conversational activities can help students become aware of the influence of their culture on their personal observations, judgments, and actions. Ideally this discovery will enhance communication between people from different cultures. *Beyond Language* can be used as a sequel to *The Culture Puzzle: Cross-Cultural Communication for English as a Second Language,* which is also designed for the intermediate or advanced level. The extensive focus on communication skills in *The Culture Puzzle* complements the focus on readings in *Beyond Language.*

In this revision of *Beyond Language,* we have changed the order of the chapters and have added topics to provide a new framework. Before being exposed to "mainstream" American cultural values in later chapters, students first read and discuss information on the cultural diversity that exists in the United States (Chapter 1). Thus, when students read "American" throughout the book, they will understand both the limitations and the breadth of the word. The previous edition presented aspects of American mainstream culture with little discussion of the demographically complex and diverse society in the United States. The new framework also provides students early in their course of study (Chapter 2) with an understanding of cultural conflict and adjustment so that they can better understand their cross-cultural experiences.

Most of the cultural information in the first edition of the book is retained in the second edition, but with updated and more extensive readings. New aspects of the text include (1) a focus on the immigrant/refugee student as well as the foreign student or EFL student abroad; (2) an early presentation of mainstream American values which are then integrated throughout the text; (3) material relevant to older as well as younger students; (4) more extensive examples of cross-cultural patterns of behavior that contrast with American patterns; (5) insight into cross-cultural reactions to expected American behaviors; (6) practical information for immigrants, refugees, foreign students, and businesspeople in the United States (for example, on succeeding in the educational system and communicating effectively in the workplace). Finally, each chapter in the new edition contains a pre-reading component and a wider range of post-reading activities.

We began writing the first draft of *Beyond Language* in 1979. When we began our revision in 1990, we realized how much more cosmopolitan English language students have become, both here and abroad. Students today have generally had much more media exposure to American culture and more cross-cultural contact than students of a decade ago. Moreover, teachers in the 1990s should be able to present cultural information more easily than before because of increased emphasis on cross-cultural understanding in teacher-training programs. Thus we have written this version of *Beyond Language: Cross-Cultural Communication* with the idea of meeting the needs of increasingly sophisticated students and teachers.

Deena R. Levine
Mara B. Adelman

Acknowledgments

To Michael, Ilana, and Kara,
for your love and patience.
   —D.R.L.

To my family members, who continue to foster
the love of differences, even among ourselves.
   —M.B.A.

We would like to begin by acknowledging the many instructors and thousands of students who have used this book over the past decade. We have received a great deal of input from students, teachers, and reviewers whose suggestions we have considered and, in many cases, implemented. The improvements in the revised *Beyond Language* are, in large part, inspired by people who know its pages well.

We would like to continue to acknowledge Dr. Ann Johns at San Diego State University for originally inspiring and encouraging us to write the curriculum that would later become *Beyond Language*. We would not have been able to complete our revision in our allotted time were it not for our assistant, Ms. Julie Bayley, instructor at the American Language Institute at San Francisco State University. In particular, we are grateful for her tremendous assistance in the pre- and post-reading activities as well as the vocabulary exercises. We also owe a special thanks to Michael Lipsett for excellent editorial assistance and continued support.

We know of no way to thank Hillel Levine for his contributions to our new manuscript. We have lost count of the hours he has spent in editing the reading texts and especially in creating new graphics. Throughout the revision he gave generously of his time and talent.

To the Teacher

The following guidelines outlining the text's chapters include explanations and suggestions intended to aid the instructor's presentation of the material. Before using this text it is important to review with the students the brief material covered in the following section, "Cross-Cultural Terms and Principles." This section lists definitions of a few words and concepts used frequently in the text. It also includes basic principles of cross-cultural learning that should be introduced to the students and reviewed with them when appropriate.

Each chapter in this text is divided into two major sections: (1) a reading passage with pre-reading, post-reading, and vocabulary exercises, and (2) conversational activities related to the topic of the reading. Endnotes and a short bibliography of books on cross-cultural communication for teachers and advanced students appear at the end of the book. The text provides material that can be covered in three to eight months, depending on the frequency of class meetings and the language level of the students.

Pre-Reading Exercises

Immediately following a quote pertinent to the reading are three types of pre-reading exercises: (1) pre-reading discussion questions that stimulate thinking about some of the main points in the reading; (2) pre-reading vocabulary, which introduces the students to key vocabulary items that are also related to central themes in the reading; and (3) skimming and scanning exercises. This last type of exercises includes reading the titles, subheadings, and first and last paragraphs of the reading as well as finding general and specific information in the reading. The skimming and scanning exercises allow students to survey the passage before reading it in order to become more familiar with the structure of the passage. More advanced students may answer the comprehension questions that follow the reading passage as a pre-test of their knowledge of the subject.

Readings

The sequence of the readings, which has been changed in this edition, is based primarily on (1) the complexity of vocabulary and language structure as well as the length of the passage, and (2) the need to expose students to cross-cultural concepts early in the course of learning. In the first edition of the book, cross-cultural conflict and adjustment comprised the last two chapters. This meant that students would not discuss these issues until the end of the course, if at all. In this new edition, we include these topics in Chapter 2 and introduce other basic topics such as cultural diversity, mainstream cultural values, and stereotypes in Chapter 1. Instructors who feel more comfortable introducing these topics after they have established rapport with their students (rather than at the beginning of a course) should present Chapters 1 and 2 after Chapters 3 and 4. We do not recommend saving the first two chapters of the book for the end of the course. Much of the information in these early chapters sets up a framework for students' understanding of their own experiences in the second culture. In addition, the American values presented in the first chapter are "recycled" throughout the book.

The readings are divided into sections that can be discussed separately if one class period does not permit the reading of an entire passage. We recommend that the instructor assign the readings as homework or, in particular for intermediate students, have the classes read the passages silently immediately before discussing them (even after they have read the passages for homework). Once the reading is completed, the instructor may wish to divide the class into small groups and have each group responsible for summarizing the content of particular sections. Alternatively, the teacher may ask students to summarize or paraphrase sections of the readings for writing assignments. The paragraphs are lettered and the lines numbered so that instructors can refer easily to sections of the readings.

Comprehension Questions

The comprehension questions are intended to help students and teachers assess whether the class has grasped the main ideas and understood details from the readings. The questions appear in both multiple-choice and open-question formats to satisfy diverse learning styles. Although the comprehension questions (and the discussion questions) precede vocabulary exercises, instructors may present either activity first. It may be more important for intermediate-level students to complete the vocabulary exercises first. For variety the instructor may wish to alternate the order of presentation of the exercises. Answers to the comprehension questions are in the instructor's manual.

Discussion Questions

These questions allow students to discuss the meaning of the reading text and, in some cases, to go beyond the text and discuss reactions to and opinions of the information presented. The questions are mostly open-ended; some of these require students to make inferences about the information presented. In addition, students are given the opportunity to discuss cross-cultural similarities and differences related to the topic of the reading. We have introduced further questions of this nature in the conversational activities section of the chapter.

Vocabulary Exercises

For each reading at least thirty words are extracted for the vocabulary exercises. In the reading these words are preceded by a small circle and are compiled in a list at the beginning of the vocabulary section. The exercises following the vocabulary list incorporate all new vocabulary words from the passage. The exercises, which vary from chapter to chapter, follow a number of formats, including synonyms, multiple choice, word forms, matching, definitions, words in sentences, fill-in, definitions in context, and phrases and expressions.

Conversational Activities

Important note for English as a Second Language (ESL) teachers and English as a Foreign Language (EFL) teachers: Since 1982 this textbook has been used effectively by ESL teachers in the United States and by EFL teachers abroad in Japan, Brazil, Singapore, Tunisia, and Australia, among other countries. Reviewers from abroad have indicated that some of the conversational activities are better suited to culturally mixed groups of students rather than homogeneous groups. Also, some of the activities require that students share information about themselves, their values, and their beliefs. For cultural reasons associated with permissible degrees of verbal self-disclosure, these exercises may not be as culturally comfortable as some of the more traditional exercises in the book. In addition, the language level and the design of the activities vary. Role-playing, for example, may be appropriate for some classes and not for others. The dialogue fill-in exercises may be more suitable for an intermediate class than an advanced one. Each chapter contains more than enough conversational activities to supplement the reading passage. Therefore, teachers should choose in advance the conversational activities that are best suited to their particular classes and to the learning styles of their students.

Cross-Cultural Terms and Principles

Note: **Do not skip this section.** Understanding the terms and principles listed below will enhance comprehension of the information in this textbook.

Terms

1. *Culture:* a shared background (for example, national, ethnic, religious) resulting from a common language and communication style, customs, beliefs, attitudes, and values. "Culture" in this text does not refer to art, music, literature, food, clothing styles, and so on. It refers to the informal and often hidden patterns of human interactions, expressions, and viewpoints that people in one culture share. The hidden nature of culture has been compared to an iceberg, most of which is hidden underwater.[1] Like the iceberg, much of the influence of culture on an individual cannot be seen. The part of culture that is exposed is not always that which creates cross-cultural difficulties; the hidden aspects of culture have significant effects on behavior and on interactions with others.

2. *Communication:* the process of sharing meaning through verbal and nonverbal behavior

3. *Cross-cultural communication:* communication (verbal and nonverbal) between people from different cultures; communication that

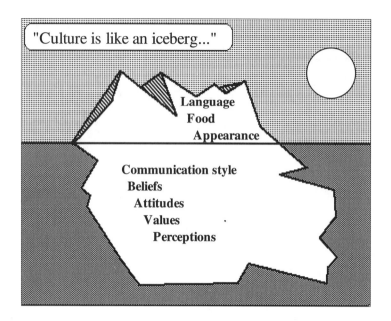

is influenced by cultural values, attitudes, and behavior; the influence of culture on people's reactions and responses to each other.

Principles

1. Culture, unlike language, is not comprised of fixed rules that apply to all members of one culture. The cultural generalizations in this text are descriptions of commonly observed patterns; they may not hold true for every member of a given culture.

2. Cultural generalizations are different from stereotypes. The latter are applied to all members of a particular culture and tend to limit, rather than broaden, one's views of other cultural groups. Stereotypes are exaggerated images and beliefs. The generalizations in this book provide insight into learned behaviors often demonstrated by many people of a given group.

3. There are no absolute "rights" and "wrongs" implied in this textbook, only cultural differences. What is appropriate in one culture may be inappropriate in another culture.

4. The textbook gives examples of many cultural patterns around the world. You and a fellow student from the same culture may disagree with the validity of a generalization. In discussing your culture's values and behavior, keep in mind two levels of observation: (1) all cultures have values and ideals that their members *say* are true; and (2) people's behavior may not always reflect those values. (For example, egalitarianism is a strong value in the United States, but in reality and practice the behavior of all Americans does not reflect this value.)

5. Culture does not explain all behavior. It does greatly influence behavior, but so too do: an individual's personality, age, gender, economic and educational levels, life experiences, relationships, and specific situations.

6. It is best not to overemphasize either cultural differences or cultural similarities. Those who say, "We are all alike; we're all human" deny the shape and flavor that cultures contribute to individual development. Those who say, "We're so different that we must stay separate" create harmful barriers by closing their eyes to what is common to every human being. We hope this textbook will encourage people to find a comfortable middle ground.

7. Finally, learning about culture is enriching. The more one learns about others, the more one sees one's own culture more clearly. By learning about contrasts, we can better understand how culture influences individuals and their communication with others.

1

Cross-Cultural Contact with Americans

"There are so many kinds of Americans that I can't tell you anything about them!"

New Immigrant in the United States

"You can always know who the Americans are in foreign countries. They have a way of walking, a way of talking, a way of dressing, and they often smile at you even if they don't know you!"

International Businessperson

Pre-Reading Discussion

1. Is it possible to describe Americans in a few words? Using three adjectives, try to describe the Americans you have met.
2. After you have answered the question above, discuss whether it was easy or difficult to think of the adjectives. Did you and the other students describe Americans similarly?

3. What are some basic beliefs and values of Americans? Give examples to support your answer.

4. When you meet people from other countries, how do you know whether their behavior is personal or cultural? For example, let's say you see three Americans who are behaving in a way that is unusual to you. How can you decide whether their behavior is typically American?

Pre-Reading Vocabulary

1. Definitions

   a. **mainstream culture**: the values, beliefs, and behavior of the dominant group in a society. The behavior of the group is basedon its values and beliefs.

   b. **individual behavior**: the actions and activities of one person

   Discussion: What are some examples of mainstream cultural behavior and beliefs in your country of origin? How do you think an American would answer this question?

2. Definitions

   a. **generalization**: a statement describing general behavior that does not apply all the time.

   b. **stereotype**: an exaggerated belief about a group often based on a lack of information or contact with members of that group

   Discussion: What are some generalizations about Americans that you have heard? What are some positive and negative stereotypes about Americans?

3. Definitions

   a. **melting pot** (literally, a pot that is used to heat things until they turn into liquid): a society in which ethnic groups blend and become one group

   b. **mosaic** (literally, a picture or design made with small bits of colored stone, glass, or tile): a society in which ethnic groups retain their separate identities but together form the larger community

   Discussion: Which do you think is more desirable: a multicultural society that is more like a melting pot or more like a mosaic? Explain your answer.

4. Definitions (Note: The terms "minority" and "majority" have two meanings.)

   a. **minority**: (i) a number that is less than one-half of the total number; (ii) a group that is not part of the larger or more powerful group

   b. **majority**: (i) a number that is more than one-half of the total number; (ii) a group that is larger or more powerful than other groups

   Discussion: Do you know what major change related to minority and majority populations is taking place in some parts of the United States?

5. Definitions

   a. **homogeneous**: made up of one group; having members that are all the same

   b. **heterogeneous**: made up of a variety of groups; having members that are not all the same

   Discussion: Is the population in your native country homogeneous or heterogeneous? If it is heterogeneous, discuss the ethnic groups that make up the society.

Skimming: For General Information

To get the general idea of the reading that follows:

1. Read the titles and headings of the sections.
2. Read the first and last paragraphs of the reading.

From your skimming, answer the following:

Is it possible to describe Americans?

Scanning: For Specific Information

To find specific information in the reading, look for clues such as certain words and numbers. Scan the reading to find the answers to the following:

1. Find the paragraph where the question, "Is it possible to describe Americans?" is answered. Exactly where did you find the answer?
2. Can a majority become a minority? To answer this question, find the paragraph with information about California in the year 2010.

Reading Text

Cross-Cultural Contact with Americans

The Term "American"

[A]   Is it possible to describe Americans as a cultural group? Your answer may depend on how many Americans you know and whether you have spent a lot of time in the United States. In either case, you may be tempted to answer simply, "Yes, it is possible," or "No, it is
5   impossible." It is a complex question to answer. There are so many types of Americans, and yet a °mainstream °culture does exist. Even the word "American" confusing. After all, America consists of two huge continents, and includes North America, Central America, and South America. Technically, "Americans" could describe, for exam-
10 ple, Brazilians, Argentineans, and Costa Ricans. The term "North Americans" is also inadequate, because it includes Mexicans and Canadians as well as people in the United States.

[B]   Unfortunately, there is no adequate word to use to label people from the United States. The term "United Statesian" is hard to pronounce and sounds °awkward. In this book, we shall use the term "American" to describe the people who were born and raised in the
5   United States. We recognize that language usage is sensitive, and so we apologize to any Americans *not* from the United States, such as Mexicans or Argentineans, who might find this application of the term °offensive.

A Description of Americans: Is It Possible?

[C]   If you don't know many Americans, you may have a mental °image of who these people are. Most likely, you saw Americans in the movies or on television. Perhaps you have met only a few Americans or have mostly just read about them. It may be that this mental
5   image is an accurate picture of some Americans. Or, it may be that the picture in your mind is far from accurate. Often, an understanding of people from other cultures is based on °stereotypes or images from the mass media (television, movies, newspapers, etc.). For example, some international tourists or immigrants in the United
10 States are not aware of the °poverty and °homelessness in this country. Some people are also surprised to see that Americans are of so many °races, religions, and educational levels.

[D]   In this book, you will be reading many °generalizations about Americans. Some people might argue that it is impossible to generalize about Americans. Americans do not come from a common

°ancestor. Except for °Native Americans (i.e., Indians),* all
5 Americans come from different °immigrant and °refugee groups.
Americans do have a common °heritage, but it is based on cultural
°diversity, or °multiculturalism. Yet despite this multiculturalism, it
is still possible to talk in terms of an "American culture."

"Melting Pot" and "Mosaic"

[E] Americans' views of their own diversity have changed over the
years. In the early to mid-1900s, some people described America as a
°"melting pot." The belief was that °ethnic groups and races would
eventually completely °assimilate and become one group. This
5 description is not very accurate, however, because ethnic groups
have always been different from one another. Many could not and
did not want to melt away their identities. Some people still prefer

*The preferred term is "Native American."

to see the United States as a "melting pot," perhaps to minimize the differences and diversity that exist.

[F]   By the 1970s and 1980s, a better °analogy was introduced: America's multicultural society was described as a °"mosaic" in which all the races and ethnic groups could be proudly displayed. Each group was seen as separate and distinct, but contributing its
5   own color, shape, and design toward the creation of an attractive mosaic. °Hyphenated terms such as "Mexican-American," "Asian-American," "Arab-American," "Jewish-American," and "African-American" reflect a general acknowledgment that cultural diversity exists, and show that a person can be an American and still maintain
10   another cultural identity.

[G]   In this textbook, we shall not describe, for the most part, Americans who belong to specific ethnic or °minority groups. However, to understand the changing face of the "American," remember that in some parts of the country, the white majority has
5   become the minority. °Demographers estimate, for example, that by the year 2010, whites and Hispanics in California will each constitute 33 percent of the population. In San Francisco's public schools, whites are already a minority. Almost 40 percent of the students in these schools do not speak English fluently. More than 20 percent of
10   New York City's population was born outside of the United States. In several other cities in the United States, members of minority groups also outnumber those who are white.

Stereotypes and Generalizations

[H] When you are describing the white, °middle class American, the African-American (i.e., black), the Asian-American, the Native American, or the Mexican-American, it is important not to rely on stereotypes. Stereotypes are exaggerated beliefs and images about groups of people and are often based on a lack of information or contact. It is easy to overgeneralize and apply the actions and behavior of a few people from a particular group to the entire group. An °individual may observe, for example, five people from one group acting similarly. If he then says, "All people from that group act like that," he is guilty of stereotyping. You can hear such comments as, "They are all like that," and "That's what they do," about any cultural group. For some reason, people all over the world °tend to divide society into "we" and "they." Positive characteristics are applied to "we" and negative ones to "they" (although some stereotypes can be positive as well).

[I]   Yet it is possible to make some generalizations about cultural groups that are true. If this were not possible, we would not even be

able to talk about separate cultures. However, we must not assume that everyone within a culture fits the generalization. Many (and often a majority) do, but certainly not all.

[J]   Outside of the United States, the °mass media does not always fairly portray members of American minority groups. For example, in certain countries, African-Americans are shown only as entertainers, athletes, or criminals. The citizens of these countries receive very little or no °exposure to the majority of African-Americans, who are neither entertainers, athletes, nor criminals. Similarly, the American media hasn't always treated foreigners or members of ethnic groups fairly. For example, the Arab has often been portrayed as either a wealthy sheik or a terrorist, the Frenchman as a "womanizer," and the Native American as a wild warrior. However, in the United States, there are now citizen organizations as well as political groups that condemn and, therefore, influence the media when a group has been wrongly represented. This type of organized reaction

to ethnic and cultural stereotypes is positive and healthy. In a multi-
15   cultural society, people must learn to become increasingly sensitive
to the needs of many ethnic groups.

Mainstream American Values

[K]   With such tremendous diversity in the United States, including
regional diversity (the North, the South, the West, the East), is it possible to make generalizations about the people of this °vast country?
Yes, it is possible. There are still mainstream values that reflect the
5   majority culture. Because of intermarriage and the natural process of
"Americanization," many people from almost every ethnic group in
America do reflect aspects of the mainstream culture. It is natural
that "Americanization" will take place. By the time an immigrant
group is in its °second and third generation in the United States, it
10   often places less emphasis on the traditional culture. After all, everyone in the United States is exposed to the same educational system,
the same political system, the same economic system, and, perhaps
most importantly, the same mass media.

[L]   There is no question that it is harder to describe Americans as a group than it is to describe more °homogeneous groups. For example, the Japanese often say, "We Japanese do this . . . ," or "We Japanese believe that . . . ." This is not to say that everyone is alike in Japan, for there are generational, political, and social differences. Nevertheless, Japan is a largely homogeneous culture with only a small percentage of minorities. It is less common to hear, "We Americans do this . . . ," or "We Americans believe that . . . ." Many Americans feel that to be grouped as one people is an insult to their sense of individualism. Yet, if Americans are compared to people in other cultural groups, definite differences in values and behavior are obvious. Many Americans, although certainly not all, hold similar values; their behavior and actions reflect these values.

A Foreign °Anthropologist's Observation of Americans

[M]   Sometimes it is difficult to describe the values or ideals of a culture from within that culture. However, if one were to look at the culture from the outside, certain observations could be made more easily. It is important to understand American values if you want to understand American behavior. Certain ways of thinking, acting, and communicating are a direct result of cultural values. The following list of values can easily describe many Americans (even a majority of Americans). For each entry in the list of American values, a "contrasting value" is given.[1] This opposite value may be found among some Americans (particularly those belonging to certain ethnic groups), but for the most part is more typical of people in other non-western cultures of the world.

American Values

[N]   1. Personal control over the environment: People can alter nature, and, to a large °extent, can determine the direction of their lives.

   Contrasting value—Fate: What happens in life is a result of a grand plan or destiny.

   2. Change: Change is healthy. People °stagnate if they don't make enough changes.

   Contrasting value—Tradition: preservation and emphasis of rituals, customs, and beliefs from the past.

   3. Control over time: Time flies. People are pressured and constrained by time because they are trying to control it.

   People shouldn't waste or kill time. They must rush to get things done. They must follow their schedules to be productive.

Contrasting value—Time walks. There is no need for people to feel so pressured. They should take it easy!

4. Equality and egalitarianism: All people are created equal. (Remember: This is a value or ideal, not a fact.)

   Contrasting value—Hierarchy, rank, status: People's roles are defined in terms of their relationships to other people; people are mostly either subordinate to or superior to someone else.

5. Individualism and privacy: Individual needs are considered primary.

   Contrasting value—Group orientation: The individual sacrifices his or her needs to those of the group.

6. Self-help: People can and should try to improve their own lives. Many middle- and upper-class Americans have the belief that people can "pull themselves up by their own bootstraps."

   Contrasting value—Birthright inheritance: People are born into either wealth or poverty; they can't change their status in life.

7. Future orientation: Look to the future and not to the past.

   Contrasting value—Past or present orientation: People should live for today or for their ancestors; they should live according to tradition.

8. Action and work orientation: Work often defines people; their identities come from what they do. (Don't just stand there! Do something!)

   Contrasting value—"Being" orientation: Work is not the center of people's identity; it is acceptable not to focus on work, accomplishments, and achievements.

9. Informality: First name usage ("Just call me Bob."), casual clothes, and the lack of formal ritual are typical in American life.

   Contrasting value—Formality: Use of titles and last names are common. People are restrained and polite with each other.

10. Directness, openness, and honesty: Honesty is the best policy. People should express themselves openly. It is not considered good to "beat around the bush."

    Contrasting value—Indirectness and "saving face": People should consider one another's feelings when deciding what to say. Honesty is not always the best policy.

11. Materialism: Tendency to be more concerned with material than with spiritual or intellectual goals.

Contrasting value—Spiritualism: The philosophy that all reality is spiritual and that nothing material is as important.

Individualism and Privacy

[O]   Let's look at a few of these values more closely. One of the °guiding principles in American society is the value of individualism, which has a long political and historical basis. This value affects many aspects of typically "American" behavior and attitudes, including
5   the attitude toward privacy. Some foreigners do not understand the American "brand" of privacy. As an example, let's look at what

sometimes happens when American businesspeople go to Japan. Their Japanese counterparts meet them at the airport, and often, from the beginning of the trip to the end, they take care of the
10 Americans, rarely leaving them alone. After a certain point, many Americans feel that they want to be alone and that they need more privacy. It is not uncommon to hear an American say something like, "They are really nice and friendly, and they take good care of me, but I just want some time to myself."

[P] Americans want and value privacy. Privacy, to an American, does not mean °isolation or loneliness. However, this is sometimes the way it is interpreted by people of different cultures. Certain languages, such as Arabic, Russian, and Japanese, do not even have an
5 exact word for privacy. It does not mean that these cultures have no concept of privacy. However, when and how privacy is expressed may be different from when and how the "American" concept is expressed. Americans may feel the need to give people their privacy or to have their own privacy at times when a person from another
10 culture might not feel the need. In some American homes, parents and children do not enter each others' rooms without first knocking. This emphasis on privacy exists because individuals feel that their needs must be respected. In contrast, in group-oriented societies people respect the needs of the group before considering those of the individual.

Equality and Egalitarianism

[Q] Another American value is the ideal of equality. Americans, unlike many people from other cultural groups, like to present an image that everyone is equal. For example, employees often call their bosses by their first names and can even sometimes joke freely with the
5 president of the company. This informal behavior and communication occur among people at all levels in the business and political worlds. Obviously, however, the company president has more power than a lower-level employee (not to mention a higher salary!). Despite this, many Americans choose not to be overly polite and for-
10 mal with a person of a higher °status. Instead, many Americans would rather think of the boss as an equal. In other words, the American tendency is to minimize status differences rather than to emphasize them.

Future Orientation

[R] Another American value is future orientation. Americans, on the whole, look to the future rather than the past. Tradition and ritual, reminders of the past, play a small part in most Americans' daily

lives. There is instead a focus on progress and change, goals that
5   many Americans try to achieve. Many people feel °optimistic that
they can be responsible for some progress and change (however
small) in their lives. This is also related to the American belief in
personal control over one's environment (and one's life), and the
emphasis on "doing" and acting.

[S]   Again, these American values are easier to understand in °con-
trast to the beliefs of cultures in which fate plays a more important
role. For example, you can often hear in Mexico, "Que será, será," or
in the Philippines, "Bahala na" (both translate to "Whatever will be,
5   will be"), and in the Arab world, "In sha'alla" ("Whatever God
wills"). Americans do not use such expressions nearly as often as
members of some other cultures.

[T]   Values such as the ones just described are the backbone of
American culture. They influence how many Americans think and
act. One challenge of cross-cultural communication with Americans
is to be able to figure out the difference between cultural behavior
5   and individual behavior, and, when you meet Americans from various ethnic groups, to decide if and how they reflect their bicultural
American identity. You will probably discover that you are continually changing and °refining your generalizations about Americans.

Comprehension Questions*

1. As it is used in this book, the term "American" refers to: [A, B]
   a. North Americans, including Canadians.
   b. people who were born and raised in the United States.
   c. South Americans only.

2. According to the authors: [D]
   a. it is impossible to make generalizations about Americans be-
      cause they are so diverse.
   b. Americans do not come from a common ancestor and so
      there is no "American" culture.
   c. even though the American society is multicultural, there is a
      "mainstream" American culture.

3. The "melting pot" view of America's diversity implies that: [E]
   a. ethnic groups were able to lose their cultural identity in
      order to assimilate.
   b. it is better for ethnic groups to retain their cultural identity.

*The capital letters in brackets refer to the corresponding paragraphs in the reading.

c. people are so different that they cannot form a single group. *many pieces*

4. As applied to American society, the analogy of the "mosaic" implies that: [F]

   a. each group can contribute positively to the society without losing its cultural identity.

   b. ethnic groups are too different from each other and will always have problems.

   c. members of ethnic groups cannot be American and also keep their cultural identity.

5. By the year 2010, the white majority will: [G]

   a. become the minority in the United States.

   b. become the minority in California.

   c. become the minority in New York.

6. Which of the following statements does not correctly describe a stereotype?   [H]

   a. A stereotype can be positive or negative, but is usually negative.

   b. A stereotype is an overgeneralization about a group of people.

   c. A stereotype is a careful observation about some people in a particular group.

7. Which statement best describes how the American media has, until recently, portrayed cultural groups?   [J]

   a. The American media has been careful not to create stereotypes about ethnic groups.

   b. The American media has always been sensitive to the reactions of political and cultural groups.

   c. The American media, like the media in other countries, has created images of certain groups that are very stereotypical.

8. What is one reason that it is possible to make generalizations about American culture despite the diversity in the United States?   [K]

   a. The same educational institutions, political system, economy, and mass media play a part in the "Americanization" of most people living in the United States.

   b. All immigrants must learn American history before they can become citizens.

   c. There are no differences among the ethnic groups, and together they form an "American" culture.

9. Why is it important to understand cultural values?   [M]
   a. Cultural values are interesting from an historical perspective.
   b. Cultural values change slowly as cultures change.
   c. Cultural values influence and guide behavior.

10. Which of the following would not be considered mainstream American values?   [N]
   a. hierarchy, tradition, and spiritualism
   b. independence, informality, and self-help
   c. egalitarianism, individualism, and an emphasis on future time

11. The relationship of individualism to attitudes and practices regarding privacy is an example of: [O]
   a. how people must change their values to adapt to another culture.
   b. how values may be different across cultures.
   c. how values affect behavior and attitudes.

12. The fact that in Russian and Japanese there is no exact translation for the word "privacy" means that: [P]
   a. Russians and Japanese do not need privacy.
   b. Russians and Japanese cannot have privacy because they live in small homes.
   c. Russians and Japanese may have a different concept of privacy.

13. The American ideal of equality means that: [Q]
   a. in the United States, everyone is equal.
   b. in the United States, the goal is equality.
   c. in the United States, employees and their bosses have no status differences.

14. People can better understand their own cultural values if: [S]
   a. they compare them with the values of a different culture.
   b. they compare them with the values of individuals from the same culture.
   c. they read about values in a sociology textbook.

Discussion Questions

Students should prepare their answers to the following questions before class discussion.

1. In Paragraph A, the authors ask, "Is it possible to describe Americans as a cultural group?" On what does the answer depend?
2. To whom do the authors apologize in Paragraph B, and why?
3. In Paragraph D, the authors say that some people might argue that it is impossible to generalize about Americans. Why is this?
4. In Paragraphs E and F, the authors discuss the "melting pot" and "mosaic" analogies in reference to America's diverse society. What is the difference between the two analogies?
5. In Paragraph G, the authors discuss some of the population changes occurring in the United States. In one or two sentences, summarize the main point of this paragraph.
6. According to the authors' statements in Paragraphs H and I, what is the difference between a generalization and a stereotype?
7. According to the discussion in Paragraph J, how has the media portrayed American minority groups and foreigners? Has this depiction been positive or negative?
8. In Paragraph K, the authors use the word "Americanization." How do people become "Americanized"? Be specific.
9. Discuss the values listed in Paragraph N. Try to give an example of at least one behavior or attitude that reflects each value.
10. In Paragraph O, the authors discuss the American value of individualism. According to them, how does this value affect the experience of American businesspeople in Japan?
11. According to Paragraph P, is American society oriented toward the group or the individual? How might this affect people's behavior?
12. In Paragraph Q, the authors discuss behavior and style of communication. Does the American ideal of equality result in formal or less formal behavior in the work place?

Vocabulary Exercises

Vocabulary List

As you read the vocabulary list below, find two or three words you already know. Give their definitions.

Paragraph A	*Paragraph B*	*Paragraph C*
mainstream culture	awkward	image
culture	offensive	stereotypes
		poverty
		homelessness
		races

Paragraph D	*Paragraph E*	*Paragraph F*
generalizations	melting pot	analogy
ancestor	ethnic	mosaic
native	assimilate	hyphenated terms
immigrant		
refugee		
heritage		
diversity		
multiculturalism		

Paragraph G	*Paragraph H*	*Paragraph J*
minority	middle class	mass media
demographers	individual	exposure
	tend	

Paragraph K	*Paragraph L*	*Paragraph M*
vast	homogeneous	anthropologist
second generation		

Paragraph N	*Paragraph O*	*Paragraph P*
extent	guiding	isolation
stagnate		

Paragraph Q	*Paragraph R*	*Paragraph S*
status	optimistic	contrast

Paragraph T
refining

A. Multiple Choice

Choose the word that *best* defines the italicized word.

1. Marie thinks that staring is *offensive.*   [B]
    a. awkward   c. acceptable
    b. rude   d. intolerable

2. Marie feels *awkward* telling Paul he is rude.   [B]
    a. uneasy   c. difficult
    b. sick   d. offensive

3. A mental *image* is something we see in our mind's eye.   [C]
  a. drawing   c. idea
  b. picture   d. thought

4. Some people believe that all ethnic groups will *assimilate*.   [E]
  a. disappear   c. separate
  b. fall apart   d. become like the mainstream group

5. There are many immigrant groups in this *vast* country.   [K]
  a. mixed   c. diverse
  b. big   d. old

6. If people do not change, they will *stagnate*.   [N]
  a. separate   c. stay the same
  b. die   d. become angry

7. Many people feel *optimistic* that there will be world peace.   [R]
  a. hopeful   c. good
  b. happy   d. wishful

B. Matching

Match the words with their definitions. Place the letter of the definition in the space next to the word.

1. _____ ancestors

_____ native

_____ immigrant

_____ races

  a. a person who lives where he or she was born
  b. people related to you in history
  c. groups of people who share characteristics, ancestors, and a heritage
  d. a person who has left his or her own country and gone to another

2. _____ diversity

_____ multiculturalism

_____ heritage

_____ homogeneous

  a. a variety of cultures or ethnic groups
  b. variety
  c. alike or similar
  d. background, history

3. _____ demographer

_____ anthropologist

a. a person who studies populations and their movements

b. a person who studies culture and the history of people

4. _____ mainstream culture

_____ mosaic

_____ minority

_____ middle class

a. a group smaller than the majority

b. the values, beliefs, and actions of the dominant social group

c. neither rich nor poor

d. a picture or design made of small bits of glass, stone, or tile

5. _____ mass media

_____ hyphenated terms

_____ generation

_____ second generation

a. words used together to express a specific idea

b. TV, magazines, movies, and radio; advertisements and communication techniques that influence people

c. about thirty years

d. a term describing immigrants who have been in a new country for two generations (sixty years)

6. _____ melting pot

_____ majority

_____ isolation

_____ status

a. position in society

b. a group with more numbers and power than others

c. a society in which ethnic groups blend and become one

d. the state of being set apart, separateness

C. Word Forms

Choose the correct word form for each sentence.

1. stereotype, stereotypes, stereotypical   [C]

a. _____ remarks can start arguments.

b. If you _____ someone, you may be wrong about the person.

c. There are many _____ about cultural groups.

2. poverty, poor, impoverish   [C]

   a. The _____ people cannot fight alone.

   b. _____ is a problem that faces the world.

   c. Should a government _____ its citizens?

3. homeless, homelessness   [C]

   a. If the government wants _____ to end, it must do something to help.

   b. There are many _____ people in downtown San Francisco.

4. ethnic, ethnicity   [E]

   a. _____ should not make a difference when a person is looking for a job.

   b. Some people believe that _____ groups will eventually assimilate.

5. culture, cultural, cultures   [A]

   a. American _____ is different from others.

   b. Behavior often expresses _____ beliefs.

   c. The authors say that there are both mainstream and minority _____ in America.

6. to generalize, generalizations, general   [D]

   a. If you only believe in _____, you may forget how to think for yourself.

   b. It is easy _____ because people tend to put things in categories.

   c. In _____, we should all pay attention to how our values affect our behavior.

7. analogy, analogous   [F]

   a. A good _____ can help people understand a concept.

   b. Being in a classroom is _____ to being in a museum; it is a place to explore.

8. exposure, expose, exposed   [J]

   a. When Chen was young, his parents _____ him to a variety of music.

   b. Chen will _____ his own children to a variety of music.

   c. Too much _____ to the sun can cause a sunburn.

9. extent, extensively, extensive   [N]

   a. The student went to the library to do _____ research for her paper.

   b. You can improve your grades to a great _____ if you study hard.

   c. She read _____ about the world economy.

D. Definitions

Choose the correct word for the definitions from the list below. Then fill in the blanks in the sentences following the definitions. *Note: You may have to change the grammatical form of the word used in the sentence.*

> individual   [H]
>
> tend   [H]
>
> guiding   [O]
>
> contrast   [S]
>
> refining   [T]

1. Definition: opposition _____

   You may understand me better if I explain my beliefs in _____ to your beliefs.

2. Definition: person; human being _____

   Every _____ is different.

3. Definition: to be likely or inclined _____

   I _____ to eat at restaurants when I am too busy to cook.

4. Definition: making better; improving _____

   If you want _____ your manners, you should start by being respectful.

5. Definition: main; leading ⸺⸺⸺⸺

My parents' advice has ⸺⸺⸺⸺ me through difficult times.

Conversational Activities

A. Observations in Another Culture

What people observe and how they interpret their observations are influenced by both culture and personal biases. When one is living in another country, the ability to observe as objectively as possible can help one understand that culture. Two kinds of observations that can be made are descriptive and judgmental. For example:

Descriptive
Many children in the United States move away from their parents at about age eighteen or nineteen. (Objective description)

Judgmental
Many children in the United States don't like their parents, so they move away at age eighteen or nineteen. (Negative and often incorrect judgment)

The purpose of this activity is to differentiate between descriptive and judgmental observations:[2]

1. Working in small groups, make a list of three to five observations of another culture.* Include observations on family, nonverbal and verbal communication, food, dress, education, friendships, and so on.

2. Write the observations on the board or read them to the class.

3. Decide with the class which observations are descriptive and which are judgmental.

4. Individually or in small groups, reword the judgmental observations to make them descriptive and objective.

---

*If you are teaching English as a foreign language abroad, the students with no experience in another culture may make statements based on what they have heard and seen (e.g., on television).

B. Cross-Cultural Communication

The purpose of this exercise is to enable you to identify shared areas of culture with fellow class members or with others from different backgrounds. When people from different cultures come in contact, the degree of shared background varies. For example, the United States and France share more areas of culture than the United States and India do. This can be illustrated as follows:[3]

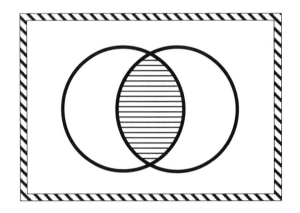

The striped area where the circles overlap represents what some people in the United States and France have in common (certain words, some foods, dress, certain values, art, and religion). The white areas represent they do not share (certain customs, styles of communication, etc.).

The United States and India have less in common than the United States and France. This can be illustrated as follows:

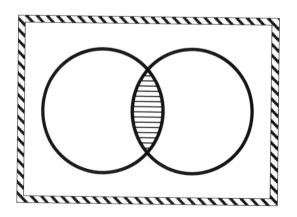

The striped area represents what the United States and India have in common (colonial heritage, political elections). The white areas represent what people in each country do not have in common (religion, communication style, family structure, dress, foods, art, etc.)

Discuss

1. What would two circles representing the United States and Canada look like?
2. How would two circles representing what the United States and Mexico share look like?

Activity: Working in pairs, make two lists showing areas in which two cultures are both similar and different. Be specific. For example, a list comparing Japan and the United States might look as follows:

Similar	*Different*
Government	Religious influences
Economy	Childraising

Discuss

According to your list, how might the differences in culture affect individuals' behavior and attitudes? Try to be specific.

C. Cultural Differences

In the previous activity, overlapping circles illustrated areas of similarities and differences related to mainstream cultures in two countries. Two specialists in cross-cultural communication have produced the following "unrefined" scale to illustrate cultural differences in another way.[4]

Directions: Look over the scale on p. 28. Read the note of explanation. Answer the questions that follow.

Scale of Cultural Differences

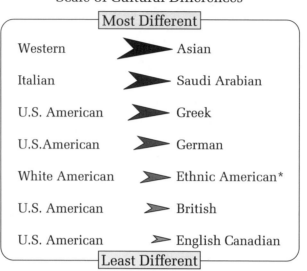

Note: We are using this scale to stimulate discussion about intercultural and intracultural differences. Students should feel free to discuss the validity of the scale. It is difficult to compare whole cultures rather than aspects of cultures. The scale, therefore, is arbitrary (or as the authors have said, "unrefined").[5] This point must be stressed.

Discussion Activity

1. Do you agree with the way the scale represents cultural differences? Be specific.
2. Draw a similar scale illustrating the following:
   a. The mainstream culture in your country of origin as compared to three or four other cultures
   b. The mainstream culture in your country as compared to several minority or ethnic cultures

---

*We have used the vague term "ethnic American" in this scale to refer to Mexican-Americans, African-Americans, etc. We do not want to imply that Americans from the mainstream society differ equally from all ethnic groups. Nor do we want to say that all ethnic Americans differ from the "mainstream" American (in fact, many members of ethnic groups have assimilated into the mainstream). The term is used only as a matter of convenience.

3. Explain your representation of the cultural differences that you have drawn on the scale. (Students in a multicultural classroom will be interested in learning about ethnic groups in other societies. Students in a homogeneous or monocultural class can compare their views.)

D. Generalizations and Stereotypes

Complete each of the following statements with the first idea that comes to your mind.

Generalizations

Many politicians are ___*demagogos*___.

Many rich people are ___*Indiferent to the poor people*___

Many women are ___*liberty*___.

Many men are _____.

Many successful business people are ___*entertainment*___.

Discuss

1. Was it easy to make generalizations about the above groups?
2. How did you form these general impressions?
3. Are the above generalizations true, in your opinion, or are they stereotypes?

Stereotypes

The difference between a generalization and a stereotype is not always easy to understand. If generalizations are rigid—allowing for *no* individuality and often encouraging critical or negative judgment—they become stereotypes.

Use the following worksheet to examine specific stereotypes.[6]

1. In the *left-hand column*, list stereotypes you have heard about people of a specific country (or countries).
2. In the *middle column*, answer the question, "Do you believe that this stereotype is true? Why?"
3. In the *right-hand column*, write the response of a person from the country stereotyped.

A sample has been completed.

Stereotype Worksheet

Stereotype	Do you believe this is true? Why?	Response of someone from the country stereotyped
All people from the United States are rich.	I don't know. I've only been in the United States for one week. I haven't seen any poor people yet. Movies show Americans with big cars and pools.	*This stereotype is false. Fourteen percent of the American population is poor, and a large percentage is middle class.*

Follow-up: International students and immigrants sometimes complain that they are asked questions that are based on stereotypical ideas, such as, "Do you have televisions in your country?" People react differently when they or people from their country are the subjects of stereotypical questions or statements. Following are some of the ways people respond to stereotypical statements or questions. Which do you think are effective responses?

1. They deny them.
2. They joke about them
3. They explain why they are stereotypes.
4. They ask why they were made.
5. They become angry.
6. They ignore them.
7. They try to defend them.

Can you think of other possible responses?

In pairs or in small groups, decide which are the most effective ways of responding to a stereotypical remark. From the stereotype worksheet, choose a stereotype and role-play a short dialogue that includes an effective response to a stereotype. For example:

Ernie: Is it true that women in your country never work?

Shelly: Where did you learn that?

Ernie: My friend told me. He was in your country for two weeks.

Shelly: Perhaps your friend only visited tourist places. It's true that not many women work in those places, because few women are bilingual. However, many women work in companies, factories, and shops. In fact, my older sister is an assistant manager in a department store.

E. Perceptions and Values

Read the following story and think about what happened. Then complete the exercise, in which you will make decisions about the degree to which you approve and disapprove of the actions of the five characters.*

---

*This exercise asks students to discuss personal feelings and values. For cultural or personal reasons, some students will feel inhibited about the open expression of their emotions. Teachers should determine ahead of time whether the exercise is appropriate.

Alligator River[7]

Characters:

Rosemary: Main character

Geoffrey: Rosemary's fiancé

Sinbad: Boat owner

Frederick: Rosemary's acquaintance

Dennis: Rosemary's second friend

Rosemary is a woman of about twenty-one years of age. For several months she has been engaged to a young man named Geoffrey. The problem she faces is that between her and her fiancé there lies a river. No ordinary river, but a deep, wide river filled with hungry alligators.

Rosemary wonders how she can cross the river. She remembers Sinbad, who has the only boat in the area. She then approaches Sinbad, asking him to take her across. He replies, "Yes, I'll take you across if you'll stay with me for one week." Shocked at this offer, she turns to another acquaintance, Frederick, and tells him her story. Frederick responds by saying, "Yes, Rosemary, I understand your problem, but it's your problem, not mine." Rosemary decides to return to Sinbad, and stays with him for own week. Sinbad then takes her across the river.

Her meeting with Geoffrey is warm. But on the evening before they are to be married, Rosemary feels she must tell Geoffrey how she succeeded in getting across the river. Geoffrey responds by saying, "I wouldn't marry you if you were the last woman on earth."

Finally, Rosemary turns to her friend Dennis. Dennis listens to her story and says, "Well, Rosemary, I don't love you . . . but I will marry you." And that's all we know of the story.

Discussion Activity

1. Rank the characters on a scale of 1 to 5 according to whom you approve of most (1) and whom you approve of least (5). Then write a sentence or two explaining your first and last choice.

   1 = most approve of   5 = least approve of

   Ranking

   _____ Rosemary

   _____ Geoffrey

   _____ Sinbad

   _____ Frederick

   _____ Dennis

First choice: Why? _____

_____

Last choice: Why? _____

_____

2. Divide into groups of four or five. Share your rankings, and explain your first and last choices.

3. Individually think about why you made your choices. Can you identify where you learned the values that caused you to rank the characters as you did? Try to write a paragraph explaining those values and where you learned them. Discuss what you wrote.

4. Do you think the values that guided your choices were personal, cultural, or both?

Interpretation of "Alligator River"

- People do not always have similar interpretations of the world around them. They perceive and interpret behavior in different ways.
- As a result of their different values, people's beliefs, behavior, and reactions are not always similar.
- No two people, even from the same culture, have exactly the same perceptions and interpretations of what they see around them.
- Many interpretations, however, are learned within a person's culture. Therefore, those who share a common culture will probably perceive the world more similarly than those who do not share a common culture.

F. Cross-Cultural Questions*

Answer the following questions about your own culture, and then discuss cross-cultural similarities and differences.

1. In your opinion, what kinds of things create the most serious problems in cross-cultural communication? Explain.

2. What kinds of cultural conflicts exist in a heterogeneous society? How are they similar to or different from cultural conflicts among people from different countries?

3. Can you think of cases where stereotypes have turned into prejudice or hatred?

4. What, if anything, can be done about harmful stereotypes?

*These questions may also be used as topics for written reports.

2

Cross-Cultural Conflict and Adjustment

"What a wonderful country. People are so friendly. I love it here. It's better than back home!"

Newcomer (After One Month in the United States)

"They do everything backwards here. I can't make friends. I feel irritated all day long. Nothing's the same. I miss my own country."

The Same Newcomer (After Seven Months in the United States)

Pre-Reading Discussion

1. According to the authors, cultural adjustment is like a roller coaster ride with many ups and downs. The quotes above show how someone's reactions to living in another culture can change over time. Explain the change in reaction of the newcomer after one month and after seven months in the United States.

2. There is a saying in English that if people feel that they do not fit in, they are like "fish out of water." Do you think a person in another culture is like a fish out of water?

3. How important is knowing the culture of a country if you already know the language? Name a few of the most important aspects of cultural knowledge that one should have before going to live in a foreign country.

Pre-Reading Vocabulary

1. Definitions

The words "to adjust" and "to adapt" both deal with changing to meet the demands of a new situation.

a. **to adjust:** to change in order to fit

b. **to adapt:** to make fit or suitable by changing or adjusting

Discussion: To what extent, if at all, does a person have to change in order to adjust or adapt to a new culture? Must an individual's personality change for the adjustment to be successful?

2. Definitions

a. **elation:** great happiness ("up")

b. **depression:** great sadness ("down")

Discussion: In which situations (in another culture) are people's feelings sometimes like a roller coaster ride?

3. Definition

culture shock: the response that an individual may have in a new country; the person may feel confused and disoriented, and every aspect of daily life may be difficult

Discussion: Going to live in another country means that a person will be "uprooted." When you plant a tree or flower and then move it to another place, what happens? Are there always problems? Are there ways to minimize these problems? What happens when a person is taken by the "roots" and moved?

4. Definitions

a. **integrate:** to become a part or a member of

b. **carbon copy:** an exact copy; the same as another

Discussion: Some people say, "When in Rome, do as the Romans do." Do you agree? Should people in a new culture try to retain some of their own culture, or should they become just like the "Romans"?

Skimming: For General Information

To get the general idea of the reading that follows:

1. Read the titles and headings of the sections.
2. Read the first and last paragraphs of the reading.

From your skimming, answer the following:

1. Is cultural adjustment possible?
2. Does cultural adjustment vary among individuals?

Scanning: For Specific Information

To find specific information in the reading, look for clues such as certain words and numbers. Scan the reading to find the answers to the following:

1. Where is the list of questions to consider when thinking about variations in people's cultural adjustment?
2. Adjustment to life in another country is a complicated process. The authors suggest that it can be a "shock" (a surprising, confusing experience). What type of shock is it? Where do the authors first introduce this concept?

Reading Text

Cross-Cultural Conflict and Adjustment

A Fish Out of Water

[A]   "A fish out of water": This expression has been used to describe someone who is living in a new culture.[1] Such a person will experience a variety of °emotional "ups and downs" lasting from weeks to years. Cultural °adjustment can indeed be difficult, and newcomers
5   adjust in many different ways. In thinking about how someone will adjust to a new culture, the following questions should be considered:

   1. °Motivation: Why did the person leave his or her native country? Did the person have a choice, or was he or she forced to leave for political, religious, or economic reasons?

2. Length of stay: How long will the person be in the new country?
3. Language and cultural °background: How similar are the language and culture of the new country to the person's native language and culture?

4. Language and cultural knowledge: How well does the newcomer speak the language and understand the culture of the new country?

5. Personality: How °flexible and °tolerant is the newcomer?

6. Relationships with others: How much support from either family or friends does the newcomer have?

7. Financial situation: What financial resources does the person have?

8. Job: Does the newcomer have a job? Is it a lower status job than the one the person had in the native country?

9. Age: How old is the person?

10. Degree of °ethnocentrism: How ethnocentric is the newcomer? Does this person think that the new culture is inferior to his or her culture of origin? To what degree does the newcomer consider everything back home to be "normal" and everything in the new environment to be "strange"?

[B]   One might predict that the easiest and fastest adjustment would be made by the flexible, tolerant person who had chosen to come to the new country and who had a job. Additionally, adjustment would be easier for someone whose culture and language are similar to those
5   of the new country. Finally, a person who has a lot of support from friends and family would probably adjust more quickly. Undoubtedly, in many cases, these would be good °predictors of a relatively smooth adjustment. However, sometimes there are surprises in people's cultural °adaptation to a new country.

Unpredictable Cultural Adjustments

[C]   Some newcomers to a society do well in their first year of cultural adjustment. However, they may have a more difficult time later. Perhaps they expected the second year to be as easy and successful as the first year, but are not prepared to deal with °obstacles that
5   arise during the second year. Those who had problems from the beginning may actually find the second year easier because they are used to solving problems. They expect difficulties and aren't surprised by them.

[D]   There is yet another unpredictable variable in cultural adjustment. Sometimes people come to a second culture speaking the new language very well, but still do not have an easy adjustment. The newcomers think that because they have a good grasp of the language, they will not have much difficulty. In addition, if people
5   think that the new country is very similar to their °country of origin

when, in fact, it is not, they may actually adapt more slowly. This is
because the newcomers only imagine the °similarity between the two
cultures. Therefore they may deny that differences exist. Cultural
10   differences do not go away, of course, just because a person denies
that they exist.

A Ride on a Roller Coaster

[E]   What happens to someone living in a different culture? The experience can be like riding a roller coaster. People can experience both
°elation and °depression in a very short period. They can °vacillate
between loving and hating the new country. Often, but not always,
5   there is an °initial period when newcomers feel enthusiasm and
excitement. The cultural differences they experience at first can be
°fascinating rather than troubling. At first, there is often a high level
of interest and motivation because the newcomers are eager to
become familiar with the new culture. Life seems exciting, novel,
10   exotic, and stimulating. However, after a while, the newness and
strangeness of being in another country can influence emotions in a
negative way. Many people in a new culture do not realize that their
problems, feelings, and mood changes are common.

[F]   When people are immersed in a new culture, °"culture shock" is a typical response. They should anticipate that they will probably feel °bewildered and °disoriented at times. This is normal when people neither speak the language nor understand the details of daily

5   behavior. The newcomer may be unsure, for example, about when to shake hands or when to °embrace. In some cases, it may even be difficult to know when a person means "yes" or "no."

[G]   After all, people can become °overwhelmed when °deprived of everything that was once familiar. The adult trying to become °familiar with another culture may feel like a child. °Stress, °fatigue, and °tension are common symptoms of culture shock. In most cases,

5   however, at least a partial adjustment takes place. This adjustment (even if incomplete) allows the newcomer to function and sometimes succeed in the new country. Certainly, there are many examples of successful adjustment among refugees, immigrants, and others who have settled in the United States. Many have made very

10 °notable contributions to American society.

From Honeymoon to Culture Shock to Integration

[H]   Reactions to a new culture vary, but experience and research have shown that there are °distinct stages in the adjustment process. Visitors coming for short periods do not always experience the same °intense emotions as do immigrants from another country. A short-term adjustment for a one-year stay in a country could be represent-

5   ed by the following W-shaped °diagram:[2]

The Adjustment Process in a New Culture

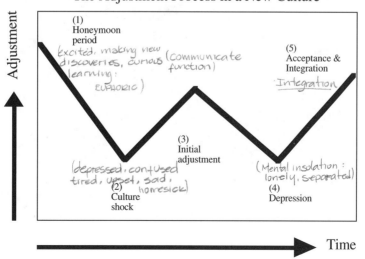

[I]   The "W" pattern of adjustment can also apply to longer stays (including permanent ones) in another culture. Each stage in the adjustment process is characterized by symptoms or outward signs °typifying certain kinds of behavior:

1. *Honeymoon period:* Initially many people are fascinated and excited by everything in the new culture. The newcomer is elated to be experiencing a new culture. Interestingly, this level of elation may not be reached again.

2. *Culture shock:* The individuals are immersed in new problems: housing, transportation, employment, shopping, and language. Mental fatigue results from continuously °straining to understand the new language and culture.

3. *Initial adjustment:* Everyday activities such as housing and shopping are no longer major problems. The visitors may not yet be fluent in the spoken language, but they can now express their basic ideas and feelings.

4. *Mental °isolation:* Individuals have been away from their family and good friends for a long time and may feel lonely. Many can-

not express themselves as well as they could in their native language. Frustration and sometimes a loss of self-confidence result. Some individuals remain at this stage, particularly if they haven't been able to find a job.

5. *Acceptance and °integration:* A routine (e.g., work, business, or school) has been established. The newcomers have become accustomed to the habits, customs, foods, and characteristics of the people in the new culture. They feel comfortable with friends, associates, and the language in the new country.

[J] Individuals experience the stages of adjustment in different ways. Some people never experience a "honeymoon" period because the °circumstances of their coming to a new country may have been too painful. In addition, certain stages last longer for some than for

5   others, depending on such factors as the newcomer's personality, age, language and cultural °competence, support from family and friends, financial situation, job status, and motivation for being in the new country.

[K]   Can a person accelerate or skip some of the more difficult stages of adjustment? Some people can, yet others cannot. This depends on individuals' ability to °cope with changes in their life. Change is easier for some people than for others. Whenever people

5   happen to be experiencing a negative stage of adjustment, they must be extremely patient and let time do its work.

[L]   How do people know that they are having problems adjusting to the new culture? Typical "symptoms" include the following:

1. Homesickness
2. Inability to work well
3. Too much eating, drinking, or sleeping
4. Anger toward the members of the new culture
5. °Glorifying the native culture and emphasizing the negative in the new culture
6. Withdrawal and avoidance of contact with people from the new culture
7. Lack of ability to deal with even small problems.

To a certain extent, all of these reactions are normal, and, in a healthy adjustment, should be relatively short-term. When these responses last a long time or become °exaggerated, the person may find it difficult to function on a daily basis. The above list is not complete. The reader can probably think of more "symptoms."

[M]   One of the most important things a newcomer can do to facilitate adjustment is to try to develop social relationships with people from one's own country, with other newcomers, and with members of the new culture. It is °essential to try to develop a group of people
5   with whom one can share new experiences. This is perhaps one of the fastest ways to begin to feel more at ease in another country.

[N]   Sometimes newcomers are eager to integrate and choose to give up their own culture. (Some people refer to this as "going native.")

Others are fearful of cultural change and °cling even more strongly to their own cultural traditions. Both giving up one's own culture and clinging to one's traditions may be extreme behavior. Studies on cross-cultural adjustment suggest that maintaining a balance between two cultural patterns of behavior and beliefs can be helpful in the long term.

[O]   If newcomers try to become aware of cultural differences and make some °modifications without attempting to change their basic personality, they will probably adjust fairly well to the new society. Especially in the United States, where there is already so much diversity, the newcomer doesn't need to become a °"carbon copy" of an American in order to be a part of the society. Newcomers can retain their individuality while becoming aware of differences. And, of course, some changes will have to be made. Feeling like a "fish out of water" shouldn't last forever.

Comprehension Questions*

1. The phrase "a fish out of water" refers to: [A]

   a. a person poorly adapted to his or her own culture.

   b. the reaction of a person living in a new culture.

   c. a person who is adjusting well to a new culture.

2. The authors mention predictors of smooth cultural adjustment. However, they also say that there can be surprises in people's cultural adaptation. What does this mean? [B, C]

   a. People who come to a country without speaking the new language fluently will not adapt as easily as those who do.

   b. Younger people adapt more quickly than older people.

   c. People can still have a difficult adjustment even if they seem to "have it all" (e.g., language fluency, support, etc.).

3. Language fluency does not guarantee smooth adjustment because: [D]

   a. language fluency is not difficult to achieve.

   b. although language fluency is needed, "cultural fluency" is also important.

   c. language fluency is the least important part of cultural adaptation.

*The capital letters in brackets refer to the corresponding paragraphs in the reading.

4. A person who is adjusting to another culture typically: [A, E]

    a. makes steady progress without having difficult times.

    b. is continually depressed.

    c. has "ups" and "downs."

5. The newness of a country can: [E, F]

    a. be very interesting and motivating for the newcomer.

    b. be bewildering and disorienting for the newcomer.

    c. both (a) and (b)

6. What are common symptoms of culture shock?   [G]

    a. fatigue

    b. tension

    c. both (a) and (b)

7. In most people's experience in another culture, what usually takes place?   [G]

    a. total adjustment

    b. partial adjustment

    c. no adjustment

8. The graph showing cultural adjustment in Paragraph H is typical of:

    a. all newcomers, travelers, and immigrants.

    b. some people who spend a year in another country.

    c. refugees who were forced to leave their countries.

9. Of the six stages indicated on the graph, which is the most difficult?   [I]

    a. culture shock

    b. mental isolation

    c. honeymoon period

10. Why might some people never experience a "honeymoon" stage? [J]

    a. They may have never married.

    b. They may have been forced to leave their country.

    c. They might have to work immediately when they arrive.

11. Why do individuals have different rates of adjustment?   [K]

    a. Because some people are extremely patient.

    b. Because the ability to cope with change varies among individuals.

    c. Because some people hate change.

12. Which of the following are "symptoms" typical of adjustment difficulty?   [L]

    a. needing a lot of sleep; being unable to work well

    b. having a lot of extra energy; finding everything easy to do

    c. criticizing the new culture

    d. both (a) and (c)

13. One of the fastest ways to begin to feel comfortable in another country is: [M]

    a. to develop a group of friends from your own country.

    b. to share your experiences with one or two individuals.

    c. to develop a group of friends, including people from your own country, other newcomers, and members of the new society.

14. To adjust to life in the United States, you should: [O]

    a. change your basic personality.

    b. become aware of differences and make some changes, but still be yourself.

    c. try to become a "carbon copy" of the typical American.

Discussion Questions

Students should prepare these before class discussion.

1. In Paragraph A, the authors say that the emotions involved in adjusting to a new culture can be affected for several years. Why do you think cultural adjustment can take so long? Why do people sometimes feel that they have adjusted just weeks after they have arrived in the new country?

2. Paragraph A lists ten variables that affect people's ability to adapt to a new culture. Can you think of others? Try to rank the items on the list in terms of their importance.

3. According to Paragraph C, why might someone who has had an easy first year in another country find the second year more difficult?

4. Explain the roller coaster analogy described in Paragraph E as it applies to cultural adjustment. Be specific.

5. Why do the authors state in Paragraphs F and G that it is normal to experience "culture shock"?

6. In Paragraph J, the authors say that not all people experience every stage in the "W" cycle of cultural adjustment. Give specific examples of groups or individuals who might skip one or more of the stages. Which stage(s) might they skip, and why?

7. In Paragraph L, the authors note some reactions to cultural adjustment that are typical but should be short-term. What should people do if these symptoms get in the way of daily life? Discuss.

8. What does the term "going native" used in Paragraph N mean, and why do newcomers "go native"? In your opinion, is it a good idea to "go native"? How do the authors describe the opposite of "going native"?

9. According to Paragraph O, do the authors think that people have to change their personality to adapt successfully to another culture? What is your opinion?

Vocabulary Exercises

Vocabulary List

As you read the vocabulary list below, find two or three words you already know. Give their definitions.

Paragraph A	*Paragraph B*	*Paragraph C*
emotional	predictors	obstacles
adjustment	adaptation	
motivation		
background		
flexible		
tolerant		
ethnocentrism		

Paragraph D	*Paragraph E*	*Paragraph F*
country of origin	elation júbilo, gozo	culture shock
similarity	depression	bewildered confundir, aturdir
	vacillate	disoriented
	initial	embrace abrazar
	fascinating	

Paragraph G	*Paragraph H*	*Paragraph I*
overwhelmed *aplastar*	distinct *distinto*	typifying *ejemplo.*
deprived *privar*	intense	straining *torcer exprimir, estirar*
familiar	diagram	isolation
stress		integration
fatigue		
tension		
notable		

Paragraph J	*Paragraph K*	*Paragraph L*
circumstances	cops *policias*	glorifying
competence		exaggerated

Paragraph M	*Paragraph N*	*Paragraph O*
essential	cling *adherirse pegarse*	modifications
		carbon copy

A. Definitions

Choose the correct word for the definition from the list below. Then fill in the blanks in the sentences following the definitions. *Note: You may have to change the grammatical form of the word used in the sentence.*

background [A]	distinct [H]
ethnocentrism [A]	diagram [H]
predictors [B]	typifying [I]
obstacles [C]	cope [K]
culture shock [F]	essential [M]
fatigue [G]	carbon copy [O]
tension [G]	

1. Definition: deal with; handle _____cope_____

   For some newcomers, it is difficult to _____cope_____ with the details of everyday life.

2. Definition: nervousness; stress _____tension_____

   If parents fight a lot, it can cause _____tension_____ for the children.

3. Definition: things that can tell the future

   Age and job status are both _____predictors_____ of a person's cultural adjustment.

4. Definition: necessary; important _____essential_____

   A positive attitude is _____essential_____ for success in a new country.

5. Definition: picture; line drawing _diagram_

    diagrams in books help to clarify explanations.

6. Definition: a feeling of disorientation and confusion in a new

    culture shock country

    culture shoc is a normal part of cultural adjustment.

7. Definition: an attitude of cultural superiority

    People who are _ethnocentrism_ have a difficult time adjusting to a new culture.

8. Definition: barriers; blocks _obstacles_

    It is important to see _obstacles_ before trying to get around them.

9. Definition: history; information _background_

    A person's _background_ affects his or her ability to do well in a new country.

10. Definition: tiredness; exhaustion _fatigue_

    If people get enough sleep and stay healthy, they can avoid _fatigue_ .

11. Definition: unique; individual; not like others _distinct_

    The authors say that there are _distinct_ stages of a newcomer's adjustment.

12. Definition: serving as a common example of; demonstrating

    typifying

    McDonald's restaurants _typify_ the American need for convenience.

13. Definition: an exact replica; the same as another _carbon copy_

    Is it possible to become part of a new society without becoming

    a _carbon copy_ ?

B. Synonyms

Choose the appropriate synonym from the list to replace the italicized word, and rewrite each sentence. *Change tense, singular and plural usage, and part of speech when necessary.*

magnify	famous
psychological	able to change
likeness	hold tightly
accepting	happiness
sadness	

1. She took her time and was very *tolerant* of her younger brother.   [A]

   She took her time and was very accepting of her younger brother.

2. Many *notable* people were at the United Nations meeting.   [G]

   Many famous people were at the United Nations meeting.

3. It is normal to experience *depression* as part of cultural adjustment.   [E]

   It's normal to experience sadness as part of cultural adjustment.

4. Getting along with people is easier if you are *flexible*.   [A]

   Getting along with people is easier if you are able to change.

5. *Emotional* "ups" and "downs" are part of the roller coaster ride of adjustment.   [A]

   Psychological "ups" and "downs" are part of the roller coaster ride of adjustment.

6. The *elation* of the "honeymoon" period may only occur once.   [E]

   The happiness of the "honeymoon" period may only occur once.

7. Some symptoms of culture shock are *exaggerated* by small troubles.   [L]

   Some symptoms of culture shock ar magnyfyed by small troubles.

8. Some people prefer to look at the *similarity* between their old culture and their new culture.   [D]

   Some people prefer to look at the likeness between their old culture and their new culture.

9. Older people *cling* to traditions, while younger people want to let go of them.   [N]

   Older people hold tightly to traditions while younger people want to let go of them.

C. Multiple Choice

Choose the word(s) that *best* define the italicized word.

1. Foreign students often *vacillate* between loving and hating their new school.   [E]   *adelante*
   a. go back and **forth**
   b. decide
   c. review
   d. move

2. Life in a new country can be *fascinating* when a person is curious.   [E]
   a. **daring** *valentía, intrepidez*
   b. incomprehensible
   c. extremely interesting
   d. extremely boring

3. In a new country, people and places are not *familiar* to you.   [G]
   a. common
   b. known
   c. easy
   d. distant

4. A new neighborhood may make you feel *bewildered*.   [F]
   a. amused
   b. confused
   c. **awkward** *torpeza*
   d. silly

5. Your cultural *competence* will improve if you make new friends from that culture.   [J]
   a. group
   b. knowledge
   c. writing
   d. **strength** *fuerza, poder*

6. If you are *deprived* of sleep, you will be tired.   [G}
   a. not allowed *permitir*
   b. desirous
   c. resentful
   d. looking forward to

7. A newcomer cannot always *adjust* quickly.   [A]
   a. resist
   b. change
   c. **retreat** *retirarse*
   d. change

8. The *initial* stage of cultural adjustment is called the "honeymoon."   [E]
   a. one
   b. last
   c. first
   d. main

D. Word Forms

Choose the correct word form for each sentence.

1. to adapt, adaptation, adapted   [B]

   a. She ___adapted___ to her new apartment quickly because she liked it so much.

      b. It is not easy _to adapt_ to a new country.

      c. _adaption_ takes time and patience.

2. to embrace, embrace, embracing   [F]

      a. An _embrace_ between close friends is common in America.

      b. In some countries, if a boy is seen _embracing_ his girl-friend, he can get in trouble.

      c. But, in many countries, it is acceptable _to embrace_ your parents.

3. glorifying, glorifies   [L]

      a. She is always _glorifying_ the United States, but I do not know how she really feels.

      b. He constantly _glorifies_ his native country and makes it sound so good.

4. stress, stressed   [G]

      a. My boss is under a lot of _stress_ because it is tax time.

      b. She would not be so _stressed_ if she worked fewer hours.

5. motivation, to motivate, motivated   [A]

      a. A good teacher tries _to motivate_ her students to do well.

      b. In high school, I was not _motivated_.

      c. In America, a person must have a lot of _motivation_ to succeed.

6. disoriented, disorient   [F]

      a. A long airplane ride can _disorient_ a person.

      b. If you are lucky, you will not be _disoriented_ for a long time.

7. straining, strains, strained   [I]

      a. When he does not wear his eyeglasses, he _strains_ his eyes.

      b. The two students did not talk for a long time, and their friendship was _strained_.

c. _straining_ to understand a foreign language all day long is extremely tiring.

8. intense, intensive   [H]

   a. Some people experience _intense_ emotions when they come to a new country.

   b. _intensive_ language courses can help people learn a new language quickly.

9. overwhelmed, overwhelm   [G]

   a. Loud people can _overwhelm_ quiet people.

   b. I was _overwhelmed_ when I first saw the Statue of Liberty.

E. Words in Sentences

Read the definition of the following words and note their part of speech. Then use each one in a sentence.

1. country of origin [D]: the country in which one is born (noun)

_____

2. isolation [I]: separation; being alone (noun)

_____

3. integrate [I]: to blend into; to become part of (verb)

_____

4. circumstances [J]: details of a situation (noun)

_____

5. modifications [O]: changes (noun)

_____

Conversational Activities

A. Cultural Adjustment Cycle

The following are direct quotes from people visiting or living in the United States.[3] Based on the information in the reading (see pp. 37–46), what stages in the cultural adjustment cycle are they experiencing?

1. "Frankly speaking, I do not feel that there are many pleasures for me in the United States right now. I am still seriously homesick, but I am getting better. I understand that this is the adjustment period. Hopefully, I will be back to normal soon. I think that when shock and frustration fade away, confidence and certainty of feeling will appear. I do believe that there are pleasures awaiting me."

   Stage of adjustment _Initial adjustment_

2. "My feelings about living in a new country are quite complicated, but I can put them in one word: 'marvelous.' Everything seems wonderful and fresh to me. You can always learn something new every minute. And you can never tell what will happen the next minute."

   Stage of adjustment _Honeymoon_

3. "When I arrived in this country I could only say, 'Thank you' and 'Good-bye.' In spite of that, I had to get an apartment. My situation was really miserable because I couldn't understand what the managers were saying. They spoke so fast that I didn't understand anything, except 'OK?' or 'All right?' I almost started crying like a child on the street."

   Stage of adjustment _Culture Shock_

Discuss

How do the above reactions compare with yours or with those of people you know?

B. Cultural Re-entry Adjustment

A cultural readjustment process occurs when visitors return to their native countries, although the stages are usually shorter and less intense than those of adjustment to a new culture. The following W-shaped diagram illustrates reactions and emotions experienced when people leave a foreign country and return to their own.[4]

As in the diagram of the adjustment process in a new culture (see p. 41), each stage in the reentry process is characterized by certain symptoms and feelings:

1. *Acceptance and integration:* A routine has been established in the new culture. The foreigner has accepted and is comfortable with cultural differences.

The "Re-entry Adjustment Process"

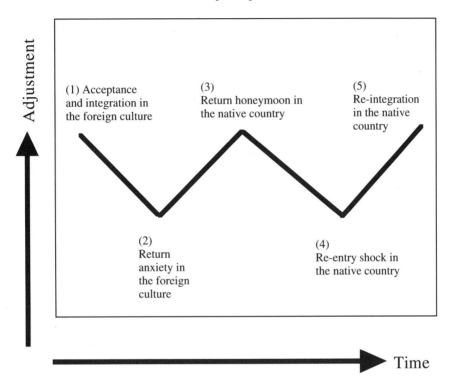

Adjustment

(1) Acceptance and integration in the foreign culture

(3) Return honeymoon in the native country

(5) Re-integration in the native country

(2) Return anxiety in the foreign culture

(4) Re-entry shock in the native country

Time

2. *Return anxiety:* There may be confusion and emotional pain about leaving because friendships will have to be disrupted. Many people realize how much they have changed because of their experiences and may be nervous about going home.

3. *Return honeymoon:* Immediately upon arrival in the person's home country, there is generally a great deal of excitement. There are parties to welcome back the visitor, and friendships are renewed.

4. *Re-entry shock:* Family and friends may not understand or appreciate what the traveler has experienced. The native country or city may have changed in the eyes of the traveler.

5. *Reintegration:* The former traveler becomes fully involved with friends, family, and activities, and once again feels integrated in the society. At this stage many people realize the positive and negative aspects of both countries, and have a more balanced perspective about their experiences.

Discuss

1. Do you know people who experienced "reentry shock" when they returned to their own country? Describe their experience.

2. In what ways is the reentry adjustment cycle similar to the process of cultural adjustment in a new culture? In what ways is it different? Refer to the reading, if necessary.

3. A refugee usually has no opportunity for "reentry shock," as most cannot return to their countries of origin. Discuss how this restriction may affect their cultural adjustment in comparison to the adjustment of international students, businesspeople, and tourists.

C. Describing Experiences in a Second Culture

1. Prepare a three- to five-minute oral presentation for the class describing your experiences in, observations of, or reactions to living in a second culture.* For example, you may want to discuss some of the following:

Experiences	Observations	Reactions
the most . . .	family life	educational system
interesting	social life	political events
educational	school life	culture shock
embarrassing	dress	friendships
important	food	other relationships
surprising	customs	
fun		

2. Select and share with the class three objects that symbolize people, places, things, abstract ideas, or cultural values in the United States and in another culture (such as your own).

D. Ethnocentrism and Adjustment

> **Ethnocentrism:** the emotional attitude, often unconscious, that one's own ethnic group, nation, or culture is superior to all others; that one's own cultural values and behavior are normal; and that other cultural values and behavior are "strange"

People can have difficulty adjusting to another culture for many reasons. One of those reasons is ethnocentrism. When people are ethno-

---

*Teachers of English as a Foreign Language whose students have never been abroad can skip this activity and go to the second.

centric, they cannot interpret cultural values and behavior except through their own cultural perspective. Sometimes people do not recognize that they appear ethnocentric to others. One can innocently say things that demonstrate a belief that "our way is right," or "our way is best." For example, someone can say, "In my country, children are much happier than in your country." How do you think the other person will respond or feel? The purpose of the following activity is to show how ethnocentrism is communicated in language.

1. Read the following statements made by people from Levadel, a fictitious country, and underline the words that convey ethnocentric attitudes.[5] Then compare your answers with those of the rest of the class.

   a. Levadelians have been very generous in teaching other people how to do things the right way.

   b. <u>Non-Levadelians do many things backwards</u>.

   c. <u>Since the only true God is the one in the Levadel culture, all other people's gods and religions are false.</u>

   d. <u>Levadel has produced the best technology in the world; therefore, it is a superior country.</u>

   e. Levadel is the best language for poetry.

   f. In Levadel, people don't talk in circles.

   g. <u>Minorities and foreigners in Levadel have to change their ways so they become like the majority of Levadelians.</u>

   h. <u>When world leaders learn to do things the way Levadelians do, the world will be a better place.</u>

2. In groups of three, choose two or three of the above statements and revise the wording so that the sentences are no longer ethnocentric. *All* group members must agree on the wording. Share your revised sentences with the rest of the class.

   Example: *Ethnocentric statement*

   Levadel has produced the finest works of art in the world.

   Revised wording

   Levadel has several superb artists who have produced well-known works of art.

E. Cross-Cultural Questions

Answer the following questions about your own culture and then discuss intercultural similarities and differences.

1. Do you think there are stages of learning a language? Do they correspond to stages in the cultural adjustment process? If so, how?

2. Do people usually change because of their experiences in foreign countries? If so, how?

3. What problems might someone expect when returning home after a long absence?

4. How might people decrease the impact of culture shock during their first few weeks or months in a new culture?

5. What is the best way to prepare for life in another culture? Be specific.

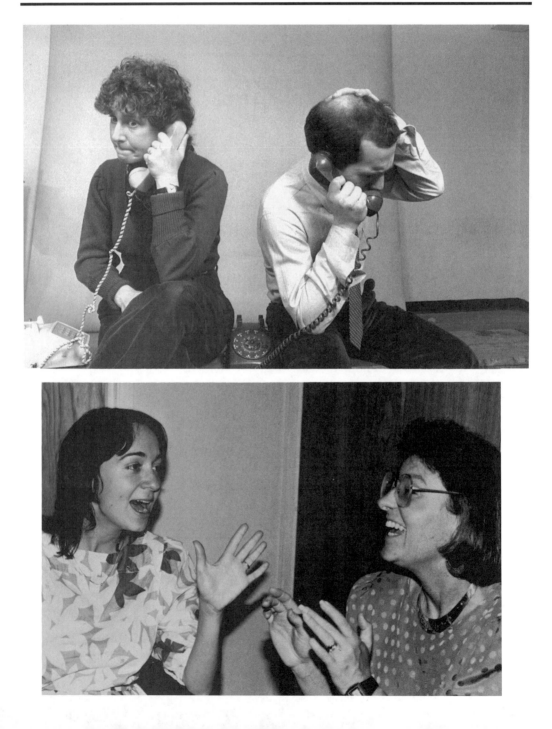

3

Verbal Communication: The Way People Speak

"To know another's language and not his culture is a very good way to make a fluent fool of one's self."[1]

Pre-Reading Discussion

1. What does the above quote mean? How do you think it is related to verbal communication?

2. What, if anything, have you observed about Americans and their way of having conversations? Is it similar to the way people carry on conversations in your language and culture? Explain.

3. In your native language, is it considered acceptable for people to interrupt each other when talking? Or, do people wait for others to finish what they are saying? What are your observations of Americans regarding interruptions?

Pre-Reading Vocabulary

1. Definitions
   a. **heated conversation**: conversation characterized by argument, loudness, a rapid exchange of words, and interruptions
   b. **hesitant conversation**: conversation characterized by politeness, indirectness, pauses, and a lack of interruptions

   Discussion: In some cultures, heated conversations are considered disrespectful, and more hesitant, polite styles of communication are preferred. In other cultures, people think life is boring unless they can get involved in heated conversations! Can you make any generalizations about the preferred styles of communication in your culture?

2. Definitions
   a. **direct communication**: a style of talking in which speakers do not avoid issues; they "get to the point"
   b. **indirect communication**: a style of talking in which speakers tend to avoid issues, hesitate, and "talk in circles"

   Discussion: Can you make any generalizations about mainstream "American-style" communication? Does it seem direct or indirect compared to yours?

3. Definition
   a. **conversation structure**: the way people converse; the pattern of their conversations

   Discussion: It is said that the structure of a good American conversation is like a Ping-Pong game. What do you think this means?

4. Definition
   a. **judgment**: an opinion, thought, or critical conclusion

   Discussion: Why do people judge others incorrectly? How do different cultural styles of communication contribute to people's misjudgments of each other?

Skimming: For General Information

To get the general idea of the reading that follows:

1. Read the titles and headings of the sections.
2. Read the first and last paragraphs of the reading.

From your skimming, answer the following:

1. Does cultural background influence styles of communication?
2. Do styles of communication vary?

Scanning: *For Specific Information*

To find specific information in the reading, look for clues such as certain words and numbers. Scan the reading to find the answer to the following:

1. The authors describe four points to consider if you feel that someone is communicating in "mysterious ways." Which paragraph has these four points?
2. What are the four points?

Reading Text

Verbal Communication: The Way People Speak

[A]   Cultures influence communication styles. Although this point may seem obvious, cultural styles can and do create °misunderstandings in conversations among people from different cultures.

[B]   For example, consider the following conversation between an Italian and an American. The Italian made a strong political statement with which he knew his American friend would disagree. The Italian wanted to involve the American in a lively discussion. The
5   American, rather than openly disagreeing, said, "Well, everyone is °entitled to an opinion. I accept that your opinion is different than mine." The Italian responded, "That's all you have to say about it?" In general, the American did not enjoy verbal conflicts over politics or anything else. The Italian actually became angry when the
10   American refused to get involved in the discussion. He later explained to the American, "A conversation isn't fun unless it becomes °heated!"

[C]   What does this example say about culture and its °influence on communication? Surely, there are many Americans who do get involved in verbal conflicts over politics, just as there are some Italians who would not become involved. However, the above conver-
5   sation °represents types of communication patterns that are related to cultural differences.

Conversational Involvement

[D]   In her book *You Just Don't Understand*, the sociolinguistic researcher Deborah Tannen discusses the °notion that people from some cultures value °"high involvement" conversation patterns, while others value °"high considerateness" patterns.[2]* Many people from cultures
5   that prefer "high involvement" styles tend to: (1) talk more; (2) interrupt more; (3) expect to be interrupted; (4) talk more loudly at times; and (5) talk more quickly than those from cultures favoring "high considerateness" styles. Many "high involvement" speakers enjoy
10   arguments and might even think that others are not interested if they are not ready to °engage in a heated discussion.

[E]   On the other hand, people from cultures that favor "high considerateness" styles tend to: (1) speak one at a time; (2)* use polite listening sounds; (3) refrain from interrupting; and (4) give plenty of positive and respectful responses to their conversation partners. Most
5   teachers of English as a Second Language (ESL) in multicultural

*Teachers should explain that these terms are not commonly used. They are mentioned here because they accurately describe an important difference in communication styles across cultures.

classrooms have observed that some students become very involved in classroom conversation and discussion, whereas others tend to participate only in a hesitant manner. The challenge for the teacher is not to allow the "high involvement" group to °dominate discussions!

[F]   The cultures that Tannen characterizes as having "high involvement" conversational styles include Russian, Italian, Greek, Spanish, South American, Arab, and African.[3] In general, the various communication styles in Asian cultures (e.g., Chinese and Japanese) would
5   be characterized as "high considerateness." Mainstream American conversation style would also be characterized as "high considerateness," although it differs °significantly from the various Asian patterns. There are important °regional and ethnic differences in conversation styles within the United States.

Incorrect Judgments of Character

[G]   Americans can have problems when talking to each other because of differences. For example, New Yorkers tend to talk faster and respond more quickly ("high involvement") than Californians ("high considerateness"). To some New Yorkers, Californians seem slower, less intel-
5   ligent, and not as responsive. To some Californians, New Yorkers

seem pushy and domineering. The °judgments that people make about regional differences within a country are similar to those they make about people from another culture. The reactions to such differences are not usually expressed in the following reasonable fashion:

10   "The way she speaks is different from my way of speaking. She must have had a different cultural upbringing. I won't judge her according to my °standards of what is an acceptable communication style."

[H]   Instead, people tend to make judgments such as, "She's loud, pushy, and domineering," or "He doesn't seem interested in talking. He's very passive and uninvolved." The people °interacting are forgetting that their respective cultural styles are responsible, in part, for

5   their °mannerisms and habits of communication. The important differences in communication create problems of stereotyping and incorrect judgments among members of diverse groups.

Directness and Indirectness

[I]   Cultural beliefs differ as to whether directness or indirectness is considered positive. In the mainstream American culture, the ideal form of communication includes being direct rather than indirect. ("Ideal" here means that the culture values this style, although not everyone

5   speaks directly.) There are several expressions in English that emphasize the importance of being direct: °"Get to the point! °Don't beat around the bush! °Let's get down to business!" These sayings all indicate the importance of dealing directly with issues rather than avoiding them. One way to determine whether a culture favors a direct or

10   indirect style in communication is to find out how the people in that culture express disagreement or how they say, "No." In Japan, there are at least fifteen ways of saying, "No," without actually saying the word. Similarly, in Japan, it would be considered rude to say directly, "I disagree with you," or "You're wrong."

[J]   Many Americans believe that "°honesty is the best °policy," and their communication style reflects this. Honesty and directness in communication are strongly related. It is not a surprise, then, to find out that cultural groups misjudge each other based on different

5   beliefs about directness and honesty in communication.

American Male-Female Differences in Directness

[K]   It is impossible to say that everyone in one culture communicates similarly. Older people often communicate according to more traditional norms than younger people, and, as mentioned, there are regional variations in the way people speak and carry on conversa-

5　tions. In addition, there are °gender differences in communication
　　styles.

[L]　　　　To generalize (and we do not want to stereotype), American
　　women have traditionally been less direct (i.e., more polite and
　　"soft") than men in making requests, expressing °criticism, and offer-
　　ing opinions. However, when talking about emotional issues and feel-
5　ings, women tend to be more direct than men. In the workplace,
　　women have learned that in order to °compete and communicate
　　with men, they have to be more direct when making suggestions, giv-
　　ing criticism, and expressing ideas. In the mid-1980s, °"assertiveness
　　training" courses were designed to help women communicate more
10　directly, especially in the business world. In the 1990s, however,

there is more recognition of the "feminine" contribution to work relationships (e.g., nurturing, interpersonal sensitivity, etc.). The emphasis in the workplace is on cultural diversity; women are defined as a "cultural group."

Cross-Cultural Implications

[M]   Americans may judge members of cultural groups that value indirectness (i.e., °hesitating, not "getting to the point," and "beating around the bush") as not being assertive enough. However, many Americans in the business world do not realize that a large percentage of the
5   world's cultures value indirectness and consider it rude to insist on "getting to the point."

[N]   When Americans go to work in countries where indirectness is valued (e.g., in Latin America or Asia), they may need to °modify their communication style. In such cultures, Americans should not be too direct when giving criticism, making requests, and expressing
5   needs and opinions. Some of the goals of indirect communication include not angering, embarrassing, or °shaming another person. North Americans working in Latin America would benefit from understanding the cultural values of "saving face" (and not causing someone else to "lose face"), and maintaining harmony. These two
10   values in personal and business relations almost always mean a more indirect style of communication. (Interestingly, although Latin American conversation style is considered "high involvement," and many Asian styles are considered "high considerateness," they both tend to value indirectness.)

Conversation Structures

[O]   Let's look at another example of how people's communication patterns differ: the way people converse. Some foreigners have observed that when Americans hold a conversation, it seems like they are having a Ping-Pong game.[4] One person has the ball and then hits it to the
5   other side of the table. The other player hits the ball back and the game continues. If one person doesn't return the ball, then the conversation stops. Each part of the conversation follows this pattern: the greeting and the opening, the discussion of a topic, and the closing and farewell. If either person talks too much, the other may become
10   °impatient and feel that the other is monopolizing the conversation. Similarly, if one person doesn't say enough or ask enough questions to keep the conversation moving, the conversation stops.

[P]   Many North Americans are impatient with culturally different conversation styles simply because the styles are unfamiliar. For

example, to many North Americans, it seems that some Latin Americans °monopolize conversations, or hold the ball too long. (Remember the "high involvement" style mentioned.) Speaking of her co-workers from several Latin American countries, one North American woman said, "I just can't seem to °get a word in edgewise. They seem to take such a long time to express themselves. They give you a lot of unnecessary details." When she talked with them, she became tense, because she found it so hard to participate. Yet she also noted that when they talked to each other, nobody seemed uncomfortable or °left out.

[Q]   The North American woman didn't know how to interrupt the Latin American conversations because North American ways of listening and °breaking in are very different. She had been taught to listen politely until the other person had finished talking. (Once again, there are gender differences; it has been observed that men tend to interrupt women more than women interrupt men.) When the North American woman did what was "natural" or "normal" for her (i.e., listen politely without interrupting), she was not comfortable in the conversation with the Latin Americans. The result was that she became more °passive in her conversations with her co-workers. The

differences between the unspoken rules of conversation of each cultural group °interfered with their on-the-job relationship.

"Ping-Pong" and "Bowling" Conversation Styles

[R]   An example of a conversation style that contrasts with the American "Ping-Pong" conversation style is formal conversation among the Japanese, which has been compared to bowling.[5] Each participant in a Japanese conversation waits politely for a turn and knows exactly
5   when the time is right to speak. That is, they know their place in line. One's turn depends on status, age, and the relationship to the other person. When it is time to take a turn, the person bowls carefully. The others watch politely, and do not leave their places in line or take a turn out of order. No one else speaks until the ball has reached
10   the bowling pins. Answers to questions are carefully thought out, rather than °blurted out. In Japanese conversation, long silences are tolerated. For Americans, even two or three seconds of silence can become uncomfortable. Americans do not like the feeling of °"pulling teeth" in conversations.

[S]   The American who is used to the "Ping-Pong" style of communication is probably going to have some difficulty with someone whose conversational style is like a bowling game. According to some Japanese, Americans ask too many questions and do not give the
5   other person enough time to °formulate a careful answer. The American, however, is not doing something "wrong" or °insensitive

on purpose. The Japanese feels that the American is °pushy and overly °inquisitive because of the difference in cultural conditioning.

[T]   To the American, the Japanese speaker appears passive and
uninterested in the conversation. The Japanese style takes too long
for the average American. The Japanese person is not doing anything
"wrong" and is not less interested in conversation. Each person has
5   misjudged the other because neither is familiar with their culturally
different conversational styles. (Conversely, to many people having
"high involvement" styles of communication, the American does not
seem pushy and inquisitive. From their viewpoint, the American
seems more passive!)

Ethnocentric Judgments

[U]   The judgments that people make about each other are often °ethno-
centric. That is, they interpret, judge, and behave in a way that they
assume to be normal, correct, and, therefore, universal. However,
"normal" and "correct" often mean what is "normal" and "correct" in
5   one's own culture. When two people from different cultures communicate, they must continually ask themselves, "Do people understand
me the way someone from my own culture would understand me?"

There may be a gap between what a person is communicating and how people are understanding the message.

[V]   People cannot °assume that their way of communicating is universal. If people from another culture seem to be communicating in what you feel are "mysterious ways," consider the following four points:

1. It is possible that the way they speak reflects a cultural style.

2. Your success in developing cross-cultural rapport is directly related to your ability to understand others' culturally influenced communication styles.

3. Your ways seem as "mysterious" to others as their ways seem to you.

4. It is often valuable to talk about cultural differences in communication styles before they result in serious misunderstandings.

[W]   It is not possible or necessary to know everything about the way a cultural group communicates before having contact with that group. It can take years to understand verbal style differences. However, if you can °anticipate differences in communication style, your judg-
5   ments about people will be more °accurate, and you will have fewer cross-cultural misunderstandings.

Comprehension Questions*

Note that this section now contains multiple-choice and open-ended questions.

1. According to the authors, cultural styles: [A]
    a. create misunderstandings in conversations between people from different cultures.
    b. help people from different cultures understand each other.
    c. are all the same.

2. How did the American respond to the political statement made by the Italian?   [B]

3. The authors say that many "high involvement" speakers: [D]
    a. consider politeness more important than verbal involvement.
    b. enjoy arguments.
    c. may think someone is not interested if he or she does not want to participate in a heated discussion.
    d. both (b) and (c).

*The capital letters in brackets refer to the corresponding paragraphs in the reading.

4. People who have "high considerateness" styles tend to: [E]

   a. speak at the same time.

   b. be polite and respond respectfully.

   c. interrupt frequently.

   d. both (a) and (c).

5. Name three cultures with "high involvement" conversation styles.   [F]

6. The authors say that the various Asian as well as mainstream American communication styles can be characterized as "high considerateness," although the two styles do differ. Is the difference significant or slight?   [F]

7. The authors suggest that Americans can have problems when they talk to each other. What examples do they give?   [G]

8. According to the authors, differences in communication can: [H]

   a. solve disagreements for most people.

   b. create problems of stereotyping.

   c. result in incorrect judgments among members of diverse groups.

   d. both (b) and (c).

9. What is one way to determine whether a culture favors a direct or indirect communication style?   [I]

10. The authors say that cultural groups misjudge each other. How does this happen?   [J]

11. According to the authors, when Americans go to work in countries where indirect communication is valued, they may need to: [N]

   a. criticize the new country.

   b. "go native" in order to adapt.

   c. modify their communication style.

12. Many Americans are impatient with culturally different conversation styles because the styles are: [P]

   a. heated.

   b. regional.

   c. unfamiliar.

13. Give an example of a conversation style that contrasts with the American "Ping-Pong" style. What analogy do the authors use to describe the example?   [R]

14. The authors discuss differences between American and Japanese speakers. Sometimes, both speakers can misjudge the other because: [T]

    a. they are familiar with the other's conversation styles.

    b. they have taken too much time to give an answer.

    c. they are not familiar with each other's conversation styles.

15. In their discussion of ethnocentric judgments, the authors talk about a "gap." What does this mean?   [U]

16. What advice do the authors give regarding judging people more accurately?   [W]

Discussion Questions

Students should prepare these before class discussion.

1. What does the example of the Italian and the American given in Paragraphs C, D, and E have to do with culture and its influence on communication?

2. Reread the list of characteristics of "high involvement" styles in Paragraph D. Based on your experience, can you add anything to this list?

3. Reread the list of characteristics of "high considerateness" styles in Paragraph E. Based on your experience, can you add anything to this list?

4. In Paragraph G, the authors say that reactions to cultural differences in communication style are not usually reasonable. What example of a reasonable response do they give? Why don't people usually respond in this way?

5. In Paragraph I, the authors state that the ideal form of communication in American culture includes being direct rather than indirect. Can you think of an example of when an American was direct or wanted you to be direct? Describe the situation.

6. In Paragraph J, the authors say that honesty and directness in communication are strongly related. Is this reflected in the American conversation style? According to the authors, what is a result of different cultural beliefs about directness and honesty in communication?

7. The authors discuss American male-female differences in directness in Paragraph K. Can you make any generalizations about the way men and women communicate in your culture? Discuss any similarities and differences regarding male-female communication in your culture as compared to American culture.

8. According to Paragraphs L and M, when should women be more direct in order to compete and communicate with men?

9. As discussed in Paragraph L, in the 1990s the emphasis in the workplace is on cultural diversity, and women are often considered a "cultural group." What do you think this means?

10. If you were to teach a class to prepare Americans to be successful businesspeople in your country, what advice would you give regarding communication, based on the discussion in Paragraphs L, M, and N? Think of three tips, and indicate which one is the most important.

11. In Paragraph O, the authors talk about conversational "games." What game does the American conversation resemble according to the authors? Describe a conversation you had with an American. Did the conversation go according to the game?

12. In Paragraph R, Japanese conversation style is compared to bowling. The authors note that long silences are tolerated between turns. How do Americans generally react to silence in a conversation?

13. The authors suggest in Paragraph T that one reason people misunderstand each other is that they might not be familiar with different conversation styles. Do you think it would be easy to talk directly about conversation styles with your friends or associates from another culture? What would you ask people from a different culture about their conversation style? Make a list of the questions.

Vocabulary Exercises

Vocabulary List

As you read the vocabulary list below, find two or three words you already know. Give their definitions.

Paragraph A	*Paragraph B*	*Paragraph C*
misunderstandings	entitled	influence
	heated	represents

Paragraph D	*Paragraph E*	*Paragraph F*
notion	refrain	significantly
high involvement	dominate	
high considerateness		
engage		

Paragraph G	*Paragraph H*	*Paragraph J*
regional	interacting	honesty
judgments	mannerisms	policy
standards		

Paragraph K	*Paragraph L*	*Paragraph M*
gender	criticism	hesitating
	compete	
	assertiveness	

Paragraph N	*Paragraph O*	*Paragraph P*
modify	impatient	monopolize
shame		

Paragraph Q	*Paragraph S*	*Paragraph U*
passive	formulate	ethnocentric
interfered	insensitive	
	pushy	
	inquisitive	

Paragraph V	*Paragraph W*
assume	anticipate
	accurate

Phrases and Expressions

Get to the point [I]   Be direct.

Don't beat around the bush [I]   Don't talk in circles.

Let's get down to business [I]   Let's not waste time.

get a word in edgewise [P]   try to say something when others are talking

left out [P]   excluded

breaking in [Q]   interrupting

blurted out [R]   spoke out without thinking

pulling teeth [R]   trying to get someone to talk

A. Synonyms

Choose the appropriate synonym from the list to replace the italicized word, and rewrite each sentence. *Change tense, singular and plural usage, and part of speech when necessary.*

habits	opinion
very important	change
shows	disrupt
confusion	forward
participate	

1. The efforts that have been made toward world peace have been *significant*.   [F]

   _____

2. Americans like to *engage* in pleasant conversation.   [D]

   _____

3. You can *modify* your behavior without changing your personality.   [N]

   _____

4. Some Japanese think that Americans are *pushy*.   [S]

   _____

5. The teacher tried to explain her lesson, but the noisy student *interfered with* her presentation.   [Q]

   _____

6. A helpful diagram *represents* an idea clearly.   [C]

   _____

7. Sometimes you can learn a lot about a person by studying her *mannerisms*.   [H]

   _____

8. Poor communication can result in *misunderstandings*.   [A]

   _____

9. Your *judgments* about people may be wrong if you do not try to get to know them.   [G]

   _____

B. Multiple Choice

Choose the word that *best* defines the italicized word.

1. Sometimes a great *notion* may develop into a successful project.   [D]
   a. movement   c. nature
   b. idea   d. criticism

2. I worked very hard, and I am *entitled to* a rest.   [B]
   a. wanting   c. deserving of
   b. having   d. due to

3. Honesty is the best *policy*.   [J]
   a. rule   c. culture
   b. idea   d. watch

4. People may feel *shame* if they make a mistake.   [N]
   a. happiness   c. shock
   b. sadness   d. embarrassment

5. If you are late, I will be *impatient*!   [O]
   a. pleased   c. intolerant
   b. furious   d. irritated

6. My friend does not say much, so people think she is *passive*.   [Q]
   a. bored   c. alone
   b. uninvolved   d. single

7. If you ask many questions, people will think you are *inquisitive*.   [S]
   a. old   c. knowledgeable
   b. a detective   d. curious

8. Sam does his mathematics homework so he will get *accurate* answers.   [W]
   a. correct   c. improved
   b. good   d. new

C. Matching

Match the words with their definitions. Place the letter of the definition in the space next to the word.

—— high involvement	a. stop
—— high considerateness	b. a conversation pattern usually typified by many words, interruption, loudness, and quickness
—— direct communication	c. able to express oneself positively; strong
—— indirect communication	d. a conversation style characterized by avoiding issues, hesitating, and "talking in circles"
—— conversation structures	e. type (either female or male)
—— regional	f. argumentative; passionate
—— gender	g. the ways people converse; the patterns of their communication
—— assertive	h. a conversation style in which speakers do not avoid issues but rather "get to the point"
—— ethnocentric	i. specific to a certain geographical area
—— heated	j. affect
—— influence	k. describing an interpretation, judgment, or behavior based on an assumption of what is normal
—— refrain	l. a conversation pattern usually typified by turn-taking, politeness, respectful responses, and fewer words
—— standards	m. hold back; prevent

D. Word Forms

Choose the correct form for each sentence.

1. interact, interaction   [H]

   a. Every time I _____ with Sue, we get in an argument.

   b. It is unfortunate that we had such a bad _____ .

2. dominate, domineering   [E]

   a. A _____ friend is one who likes power.

   b. I do not want my father to _____ tonight's dinner conversation.

3. honestly, honesty, honest   [J]

   a. _____ is a good idea, but it is not always possible.

   b. Please be _____ and tell me if you like my new car.

   c. _____ , I have no preferences. Either tea or coffee is fine.

4. to criticize, criticism, critic   [L]

   a. Constructive _____ can help a person improve.

   b. A _____ is a person who reviews movies, food, or restaurants.

   c. If you are going _____ me, please do it nicely.

5. compete, competition   [L]

   a. I will _____ in this weekend's tennis tournament, if the weather is good.

   b. The _____ should be exciting, because several famous people will be there!

6. monopolize, monopolizing   [O]

   a. When people _____ , they take total control of a situation.

   b. Stop _____ this discussion if you want to be fair.

7. formulate, formula   [S]

   a. The student failed the math exam because he forgot the

   _____ .

   b. In class, it is a good idea to take your time to _____ a good question.

8. assume, assumptions, assuming   [V]

   a. People who make _____ about other people before they meet them will probably be wrong.

   b. I am _____ that you have your homework with you.

   c. _____ nothing, and you may be pleasantly surprised.

9. insensitive, insensitivity   [S]

   a. If you are _____ , you might hurt someone's feelings.

   b. Tom's rude comments showed his _____ toward other cultural groups.

10. anticipate, anticipation, anticipating   [W]

   a. I am waiting for a response with great _____ .

   b. The students are _____ a challenging examination.

   c. My mother did not _____ such a big birthday party.

11. hesitating, hesitant, hesitates   [M]

   a. He who _____ loses his chance.

   b. All day yesterday, my friend was _____, but she finally made the decision to study abroad.

   c. Conversation that is characterized by indirectness and politeness can be called _____ conversation.

E. Phrases and Expressions

Which statement *best* conveys the meaning of the *italicized* words?

1. A person who *beats around the bush* when asking a favor: [I]
   a. asks directly.
   b. asks indirectly.
   c. doesn't ask at all.

2. Someone who says, *"Don't just blurt out your answer; think first!"* means that: [R]
   a. you should not give away your answer.
   b. you should guess at an answer.
   c. you should not speak without thinking.

3. A helpful police officer who says, *"Get to the point,"* means: [I]
   a. give me many details about your story.
   b. give me the story in as few words as possible.
   c. give me the knife with the sharpest point.

4. Someone who says that getting your opinion about politics is like *pulling teeth* means that: [R]
   a. it is extremely difficult to get your opinion.
   b. it is very painful to get your answer.
   c. it is difficult to make an appointment to get your answer.

Conversation Activities

A. **Rules of Speaking**

In language, there are unspoken rules of speaking. These rules exist in every language, but differ significantly from culture to culture. The rules have to do with permissible degrees of directness, politeness, and formality, and they affect many of the functions of communication. The following communication functions are common to all languages, but their expression can be very different across cultures.

Activity: Read the list of communication functions below and choose one. In your *native language*, write a short dialogue containing that function. Then translate the dialogue *word for word* into English. Find out from your teacher (or any American) if the translation sounds correct. For variety, students in the class should choose different functions to translate. From the direct translations, you should be able to see how culture affects the way we speak.

Communication Functions

praise	compliment	evaluate
criticize	request	demand
inquire	clarify	correct
give feedback	receive feedback	interrupt
offer	refuse	maintain conversation
disagree	disapprove	agree
express emotion	extend invitations	initiate conversations
end conversations		

Follow-up: If your class is multicultural, compare the various ways different languages express the above functions of communication.

B. **"Small Talk"**

Conversation often begins with "small talk." Small talk is important because it often helps to maintain conversations (i.e., keep them going), and it can lead to interesting discussions. In an introductory meeting, maintaining a conversation is easier when two people find that they have something in common. In the following dialogue, the speakers use small talk (including questions) to discover what they have in common. Notice the "Ping-Pong" structure of the conversation.

> *Sue:* It's nice to meet you. My friend told me about you. Have you lived in Seattle long?

Mark: No, only three months. How about you?

Sue: I moved here three years ago from California.

Mark: Oh really! I'm from California too. Where did you live in California?

Sue: In Gilroy, not far from San Jose.

Mark: This is really a *coincidence*. I'm from Gilroy, too! I like telling people I'm from the garlic capital of the world. Did you usually go to the summer garlic festival?

Sue: I used to go every summer. How about you?

Mark: I went to most of them. I thought the one in 1980 was great. Did you go to that one?

In this conversation, Sue and Mark asked each other "small talk" questions before they found that they had a common background. Once they discovered this, the conversation flowed easily.

Appropriate Questions for Initial Small Talk

1. How long have you lived here?
2. Have you always lived in (for example) New York?
3. Do you like living here?
4. What are you studying? (to a student)
5. What do you do? (or) What is your line of work?
6. What do you think of the weather we've been having?

Inappropriate Questions for Initial Small Talk

1. Are you married?
2. How much money do you earn?
3. How much did you pay for your car?
4. What is your religion?
5. Are you a Republican or a Democrat?

Discuss

1. In your culture, what questions are considered unacceptable for conversation?
2. What are common questions that people ask in initial conversations?

A lot of small talk is "situational." That is, people initiate a conversation about their common situation. This is often a starting point for further conversation. For example:

At a party: "How do you know Deena?"

At a film: "Do you go to see international films often?"

At a university lecture: "What did you think of Professor Adelman's talk?"

C. Initiating and Maintaining Conversations

Initiating and maintaining conversations are necessary skills when one is learning a new language. In English, one of the best ways of initiating and maintaining a conversation is for at least one of the speakers to ask the other questions. Read the following conversation, and discuss the problem with it.

(Rick sees Debbie at a party and decides he would like to get to know her.)

   Rick: Hello. Where are you from?

Debbie: From New York.

   Rick: Why did you come to California?

Debbie: To study.

   Rick: Oh, what are you studying?

Debbie: Architecture.

   Rick: How long do you plan to stay here?

Debbie: Two years.

   Rick: When did you come?

Debbie: Three weeks ago.

(Rick is already feeling frustrated. He decides it is not worth getting to know Debbie.)

1. Following is the same dialogue between Debbie and Rick. Change it so that it is not one-sided by adding a question or a comment after Debbie's short answers. Write in Rick's responses to Debbie's questions.

   Rick: Hello. Where are you from?

Debbie: From New York. _____

_____

   Rick: _____

Why did you come to California?

Debbie: To study. _____

_____

Rick: _____

What are you studying?

Debbie: Architecture. _____

_____

Rick: _____

How long do you plan to stay here?

Debbie: Two years. _____

Rick: _____

When did you come?

Debbie: Three weeks ago. _____

Another way of maintaining a conversation is to add extra information to a one-word response. In the following conversation, Judi helps to maintain the conversation by giving more than a one- or two-word response.

(Judi and Char have just met and have exchanged names.)

Char: Where do you work?

Judi: I work at the university in San Diego. I'm a computer operator.

Char: How's the weather in San Diego? I'm from San Francisco.

Judi: It's warm most of the time. For the past two winters, we've had a lot of rain.

2. In the following dialogue, a student is discussing language learning with her teacher. Add extra information to the teacher's one-word responses.

Mari: Do you think that learning a foreign language is difficult?

Ms. Sofia: Yes. _____

_____

_____

Mari: Are some languages easier to learn than others?

Ms. Sofia: Yes. _____

_____

_____

Mari: Should children in elementary school be required to study foreign languages?

Ms. Sofia: Yes. _____

_____

_____

D. Informality/Formality

In English, as in other languages, the types of vocabulary, structure, and tone used in conversation vary with the situation. In each of the following examples, compare the ways that a request may be made, and look at the vocabulary used and the length of the sentence:

I'm sorry to trouble you, but could you please tell me where the library is?   (*formal*)

Would you be so kind as to tell me where the library is? (*formal*)

Where is the library, please?   (*semiformal*)

Where's the library?   (*informal*)

Learning different conversation styles in a second language is not always easy. It is necessary to know how to vary speech according to situations. Read the following situations, and respond to each appropriately:

1. There are discipline problems in one of your classes. Students are talking all the time, and you can't hear the teacher or concentrate on the subject. You feel you must say something about the situation to your teacher. You also want to speak to the talkative students.

   a. What would you say after class to your teacher?
      Please Teacher I have to say something to you about class problem with the partners

   b. What would you say to the other students?
      Please Be quiet, because I need concentrate on the subject

2. You need some money and are considering asking either some relatives or a friend for a loan.

    a. How would you ask your relatives? *Could you please make me a loan?*

    b. How would you ask a friend?

3. You have just read an excellent article written by a student you know and a professor whom you don't know very well. You would like to compliment both of them.

    a. What would you say to the student? *That's good article*

    b. What would you say to the professor? *I like your article congratulations!!!*

Follow-up: Look again at the above three situations and determine how you would respond in your *native language*. How formal and informal would you be? In your language, what words or grammatical constructions indicate formality and informality? How direct or indirect would you be?

E. Multiple-Choice Questionnaire

The following questions are intended to stimulate cross-cultural discussion and to help you become familiar with American customs and responses in the area of verbal communication. First, write an answer that describes a likely response in your country. On the multiple-choice questions, try to guess what an American would do. *More than one answer may be correct.*

1. When someone compliments the watch you are wearing, you would:

In your country: *Thank you*

In the United States:

a. Say, "Oh this cheap thing? It's not worth much."

b. Give it to him.

c. Say, "Thanks," and smile.

d. Say, "Would you like to have it?"

2. It is not considered appropriate to give compliments to:

In your country: _____

In the United States:

a. A woman about her husband.

b. A man about his wife.

c. A couple about their child.

d. A doctor about his or her salary.

3. To which of the following statements would you respond "thank you"?

In your country: _____

In the United States:

a. "You are a clever person."

b. "Let me open the door for you."   *thank you*

c. "Your face is beautiful."

d. "Please accept this gift as a symbol of our deep friendship."
   thank you

4. Someone who wanted to criticize the behavior of a fellow student would:

In your country: _____

In the United States:

a. Say something to the student in front of the class.

b. Tell the teacher to speak to the student.

c. Speak to the student after class.

5. If students want to criticize the way a professor teaches, they should:

In your country: _____

In the United States:

a. Go directly to the dean of the department.

b. Ask the professor for an appointment to talk about the class.

c. Go directly to the professor's office with several other students and state the complaint.

d. Complain to the professor during class time.

6. What would be a polite way to evade a question that you don't want to answer (e.g., "What do you think of the government in your country?")?

In your country: _____

In the United States:

a. "It's none of your business."

b. "I refuse to answer that question."

c. "That question is inappropriate, so I can't answer it."

d. "Oh, I don't know. I'm not very interested in politics."

7. If someone uses a foreign word or phrase you don't know, you might:

In your country: _____

In the United States:

a. Say, "Please repeat."

b. Say, "I'm sorry, I didn't understand what you said. Could you please repeat that last sentence (or word)?"

c. Say nothing and pretend that you have understood.

d. Say, "Excuse me, but what does that sentence (or word) mean?"

8. If someone gives you directions in a second language so quickly that you don't understand, you might respond:

In your country: _____

In the United States:

a. "Could you repeat that?"

b. "Thank you. I appreciate your help."

c. "Excuse me, I'm still learning the language. Could you repeat that a little more slowly?"

d. Try to repeat the directions to the person.

9. If someone offers you food that you really don't like, you might say:

In your country: _____

In the United States:

a. "I hate that."

b. "Sure, I'd love some more."

c. "I'll have just a little bit, please."

d. "Thanks, but I'm really full."

10. You have just been asked out to dinner, but you really don't want to go with the person who invited you. You might say:

In your country: _____

In the United States:

a. "Thanks a lot, but I'm busy tonight."

b. "No, I really don't enjoy being with you."

c. "I'm dieting, so I mustn't go out to eat."

d. "I don't think so. I already have plans."

11. When asking your neighbors to lower the volume of their stereo, you might say:

In your country: _____

In the United States:

a. "Turn the music down."

b. "Would you mind turning the music down? I'm studying."

c. "You are very rude."

d. "If you don't turn your stereo down, I'll turn mine up."

12. When introduced to a man your age or younger, what would you say?

In your country: _____

In the United States:

a. "How do you do?"

b. "Pleased to meet you," and lightly embrace him.

c. "Pleased to meet you," and shake his hand.

d. Say nothing and shake his hand.

13. When introduced to a woman your age or younger, what would you say?

In your country: _____

In the United States:

a. "How do you do?"

b. "Pleased to meet you," and kiss her on the cheek.

c. "Pleased to meet you."

d. "Nice to meet you," and shake her hand.

14. When introducing yourself to someone you don't know at a party, what would you say?

In your country: _____

In the United States:

a. "Hi, I'm ___H. B.___. What's your name?"

b. "May I introduce myself to you, and at the same time may I make your (acquaintance?") *May I get introduce you ?*

c. "Hi. I'd like to meet you."

d. "Hi. I'm ___H. B.___. Do you know many people here?"

15. Which topics are inappropriate to discuss immediately after an introduction?

In your country: _____

In the United States:

a. Marital status

b. Religion

c. Age

d. Occupation

F. Cross-Cultural Questions*

Answer the following questions about your own culture, and then discuss cross-cultural similarities and differences.

1. When do you use first names in introductions?

2. When do you use titles (e.g., Mr., Miss, etc.) in introductions?

3. What else might you explain to Americans about introductions in your country?

4. What does silence indicate in conversations? Does it always indicate the same thing (e.g., approval or disapproval)?

5. Is it acceptable to interrupt others? If so, when?

6. Who can criticize whom? Under what circumstances? In what manner do people make criticisms?

7. How do people refuse invitations? Is it appropriate to insist that people accept an invitation if they have refused several times?

*These questions may also be used as topics for written reports.

I have another commitment.

compliment (cumplido
(opposite criticism)

8. How frequently do people compliment each other (e.g., husbands and wives, parents and children, teachers and students)? Which is the expected way to respond to a compliment? (For example, "Thank you," or "Oh, no. It's not true.")

Cultural Notes

1. In a formal introduction, Americans often use titles until they are told they may use first names.

2. When two people are introduced by a third person, the first and last names are usually given. For example:

   A friend: Michael, I'd like you to meet my friend, Diane Rae. Diane, I'd like you to meet Michael Lipsett.

   Note: In less formal introductions, last names may be dropped.

3. The following is a list of titles used in introductions and conversations. (Except when noted, these titles are followed by a person's last name.)

Dr. (Doctor)	Used to address medical doctors (M.D.) and university professors who have earned a doctorate (Ph.D.)
Prof. (Professor)	Used to address a college or university teacher
Teacher	Used by very young children in school (*Note:* The word "teacher" is not usually followed by a name.)
Mrs.	Used to address a married woman (teacher, director, etc.)
Miss	Used to address an unmarried woman (teacher, waitress, businesswoman, etc.)
Ms.	Used to address an unmarried or married woman (teacher, housewife, professional, etc.)
Mr.	Used to address a man (teacher, business man,etc.)

4. The following phrases may be used if a name given in an introduction is not understood or is forgotten:

Informal

> Excuse me, I didn't catch your name.
>
> I'm sorry, what is your name again?
>
> Could you spell your first name? That will help me pronounce it better.

Formal

> May I please have your name again?
>
> Would you please repeat your name?

5. Generally, when Americans extend invitations, they prefer to know the response ("Yes, I can come," or "No, I can't come") soon after an invitation is made. This is particularly true of dinner and other formal invitations.

6. Complimenting can be a way of initiating conversation (e.g., "Hi, how are you? Those are beautiful earrings that you're wearing. Where are they from?"). It is acceptable to compliment a person's material possessions (e.g., home, decorations in the home, clothes, etc.). Too many compliments, however, may be interpreted as insincerity. On the other hand, not enough compliments may be interpreted as a sign of apathy or dislike. For example, if a guest doesn't praise the quality of a dinner, the host might feel that the guest didn't like it.

7. In some parts of the world, people believe that compliments are dangerous because they invite the "evil eye" (bad luck), and, therefore, compliments are not given freely. In the mainstream culture, this belief does not exist. There are no restrictions or superstitions related to giving compliments.

8. There are several ways of requesting information in English. Note the differences between the informal and formal language.

Informal

> *Can* you give me directions to the city library, *please?*
>
> *Where* is the cafeteria, *please?*
>
> *Do* you have any information on universities in northern California?

Formal

> *Excuse me, may* I ask you a question?
>
> *Pardon me, may* I interrupt you for a moment to ask you a question?

Excuse me, would you *mind* closing the window (e.g., in a bus)?

9. In English, favors may be requested either informally or formally. Often a request for an important favor is more formal than a request for a less important one:

Informal

Can I borrow your pen?

Would you lend me your library card?

Do you *have* an extra notebook that I could use?

Do you *mind* if I return your book next week?

Formal

May I *please* have a few extra days to complete my term paper?

Would you *mind* giving me that information?

Very Formal

Would you be kind enough to direct me to the university library?

May I ask you a favor? Would you mind contacting my parents when you're in my country?

Would you consider allowing me two weeks of vacation instead of one?

Would it be at all possible to borrow your car?

10. There are many ways of ending conversations and leaving someone before the final good-bye. Here are a few examples:

Informal

OK. Good talking to you.

Yeah. I hope to see you around.

Take care.

See you later.

Formal

It was very nice talking to you.

I hope we'll meet again soon.

I do too. That would be nice.

Good-bye.

11. The following are some expressions of farewell:

Informal
  Have a nice day.
  Enjoy your weekend.
  See ya around.
  So long.
  Bye-Bye.
  Bye.

Formal
  Good-bye.
  It was nice meeting you.
  Have a nice evening (day, week, etc.).

Supplementary Vocabulary and Phrases

  to make the acquaintance of
  to be on a first-name basis with
  "How do you do?" (formal)
  "(I'm) Pleased to meet you."
  "(It's) Nice to meet you."
  "I'm happy to meet you."

to request	to apologize	to refuse
to demand	to boast	to give an opinion
to criticize	to brag	to suggest an idea
	to protest	to excuse oneself
	to agree	to congratulate

4

Nonverbal Communication: Speaking Without Words

"Culture hides much more than it reveals, and strangely enough, what it hides, it hides most effectively from its own participants."[1]

Pre-Reading Discussion

1. Can you think of what culture hides in the area of nonverbal communication? What does the last part of the above quote mean: "What it hides, it hides most effectively from its own participants"?

2. What are some of the ways that people communicate without using words? Compare your answers with those of other students.

3. In your culture, how close do you stand to people when you are talking to them? Demonstrate the distance. Do you think this space differs across cultures?

Pre-Reading Vocabulary

1. Definitions
   a. **verbal communication**: spoken communication, including the use of words and intonation to convey meaning
   b. **nonverbal communication**: "silent" communication, including the use of gestures, facial expressions, eye contact, and conversational distance

   Discussion: Do you depend very much on nonverbal language to communicate? Or is most of your meaning conveyed through verbal communication? Can you make any cultural generalizations regarding the degree of verbal and nonverbal communication that people use?

2. Definition

   universal: global, worldwide

   Discussion: What types of nonverbal communication do you think are universal? For example, do you think the smile, eye contact, or facial expressions have the same functions across cultures?

3. Definition

   gesture: movement of the body or part of the body, especially the hands

   Discussion: From your observations of Americans, do you think that they "talk" a lot with their hands? Have you noticed differences among Americans from various ethnic groups?

Skimming: For General Information

To get the general idea of the reading that follows:

1. Read the titles and headings of the sections.
2. Read the first and last paragraphs of the reading.

From your skimming, answer the following:

1. Do members of all cultures have the same nonverbal communication?
2. Where in the reading is the answer stated?

Scanning: For Specific Information

To find specific information in the reading, look for clues such as certain words and numbers. Scan the reading to find the answers to the following:

1. In which paragraph do the authors quote a research study that gives the percentage of nonverbal communication used in conveying attitudes? What is the percentage?
2. In which paragraph do the authors mention a specific conversation distance that is common among Americans? What is the distance?

Reading Text

Nonverbal Communication: Speaking Without Words

"He didn't look at me once. I know he's guilty. Never trust a person who doesn't look you in the eye."

American Police Officer

"Americans smile at strangers. I don't know what to think of that."

Russian Engineer

"Americans seem cold. They seem to get upset when you stand close to them."

Jordanian Teacher

[A]   The American police officer, the Russian engineer, and the Jordanian teacher made these comments about interactions they had with someone from a different culture. Their comments demonstrate how people can °misinterpret °nonverbal communication that is culturally
5   different from their own. Of course, this can also happen in conversation among individuals of the same cultural background, but it does not usually happen as often or to the same degree. Many people think that all they really need to pay attention to in a conversation is the spoken word. This is far from the truth!

[B]   Language studies traditionally °emphasized verbal and written communication. Since about the 1960s, however, researchers seriously began to consider what takes place without words in conversations. In some instances, more nonverbal than verbal communication

5   occurs. For example, if you ask an obviously depressed person, "What's wrong?" and he answers, "Nothing, I'm fine," you probably won't believe him. Or when an angry person says, "Let's forget this subject. I don't want to talk about it anymore!" she hasn't stopped communicating. Her silence and °withdrawal continue to °convey
10   emotional meaning.

[C]   One study done in the United States showed that 93 percent of a message was °transmitted by the speaker's tone of voice and facial expressions. Only 7 percent of the person's attitude was conveyed by words.[2] Apparently, we express our emotions and attitudes more
5   nonverbally than verbally.

Cultural Differences in Nonverbal Communication

[D]   Nonverbal communication expresses meaning or feeling without words. °Universal emotions, such as happiness, fear, and sadness, are expressed in a similar nonverbal way throughout the world. There are, however, nonverbal differences across cultures that may be a
5   source of confusion for foreigners. Let's look at the way people express sadness. In many cultures, such as the Arab and Iranian cultures, people express grief openly. They °mourn out loud, while people from other cultures (e.g., China and Japan) are more °subdued. In

Asian cultures, the general belief is that it is unacceptable to show
10 emotion openly (whether sadness, happiness, or pain).

[E]   Let's take another example of how cultures differ in their nonverbal expression of emotion. Feelings of friendship exist everywhere
in the world, but their expression varies. It is acceptable in some
countries for men to embrace and for women to hold hands; in other
5 countries, these displays of °affection are discouraged or prohibited.

[F]   As with verbal communication, what is considered usual or
polite behavior in one culture may be seen as unusual or impolite in
another. One culture may °determine that snapping fingers to call a
waiter is appropriate, whereas another may consider this gesture
5 rude. We are often not aware of how gestures, facial expressions, eye
contact, and the use of conversational distance affect communication.
To interpret another culture's style of communication, it is necessary
to study the "silent language"[3] of that culture.

Gestures and Body Positioning

[G]   °Gestures are specific body movements that carry meaning. Hand
motions alone can convey many meanings: "Come here," "Go away,"

"It's O.K.," and "That's expensive!" are just a few examples. The gestures for these phrases often differ across cultures. For example,
5   °beckoning people to come with the palm up is common in the United States. This same gesture in the Philippines, Korea, and parts of Latin America as well as other countries is considered rude. In some countries, only an animal would be beckoned with the palm up.

[H]   As children, we °imitate and learn to use these nonverbal movements to °accompany or replace words. When traveling to another country, foreign visitors soon learn that not all gestures are universal. For example, the "O.K." gesture in the American culture is a symbol
5   for money in Japan. This same gesture is °obscene in some Latin American countries. (This is why the editors of a Brazilian newspaper enjoyed publishing a picture of a former American president giving the "O.K." symbol with both hands!)

[I]   Many American business executives enjoy relaxing with their feet up on their desks. But to show a person from Saudi Arabia or Thailand the sole of one's foot is extremely insulting, because the foot is considered the dirtiest part of the body. Can you imagine the
5   reaction in Thailand when a foreign shoe company °distributed an advertisement showing a pair of shoes next to a sacred sculpture of Buddha?

Facial Expressiveness

[I]   Facial expressions carry meaning that is determined by situations and relationships. For instance, in American culture the smile is typically an expression of pleasure. Yet it also has other functions. A woman's smile at a police officer does not carry the same meaning as the smile she gives to a young child. A smile may show affection, convey politeness, or °disguise true feelings. It also is a source of confusion across cultures. For example, many people in Russia consider smiling at strangers in public to be unusual and even °suspicious behavior. Yet many Americans smile freely at strangers in public places (although this is less common in big cities). Some Russians believe that Americans smile in the wrong places; some Americans believe that Russians don't smile enough. In Southeast Asian cultures, a smile is frequently used to cover emotional pain or embarrassment. Vietnamese people may tell the sad story of how they had to leave their country but end the story with a smile.

Our faces reveal emotions and attitudes, but we should not attempt to "read" people from another culture as we would "read" someone from our own culture. The degree of facial °expressiveness one °exhibits varies among individuals and cultures. The fact that members of one culture do not express their emotions as openly as do members of another does not mean that they do not experience emotions. Rather, there are cultural restraints on the amount of nonverbal

expressiveness permitted. For example, in public and in formal situations many Japanese do not show their emotions as freely as
10 Americans do. More privately and with friends, Japanese and Americans seem to show their emotions similarly. Many teachers in the United States have a difficult time knowing whether their Japanese students understand and enjoy their lessons. The American teacher is looking for more facial °responsiveness than what the
15 Japanese student is comfortable with in the classroom situation.

[L]   It is difficult to generalize about Americans and facial expressiveness because of individual and ethnic differences in the United States. People from certain ethnic backgrounds in the United States tend to be more facially expressive than others. The key, is to try not
5 to judge people whose ways of showing emotion are different. If we judge according to our own cultural norms, we may make the mistake of "reading" the other person incorrectly.

Eye Contact

[M]   Eye contact is important because °insufficient or °excessive eye contact can create communication barriers. In relationships, it serves to show °intimacy, attention, and influence. As with facial expressions, there are no specific rules governing eye behavior in the United
5 States, except that it is considered rude to stare, especially at strangers. In parts of the United States, however, such as on the West

Coast and in the South, it is quite common to °glance at strangers when passing them. For example, it is usual for two strangers walking toward each other to make eye contact, smile, and perhaps even
10 say, "Hi," before immediately looking away. This type of contact doesn't mean much; it is simply a way of acknowledging another person's °presence. In general, Americans make less eye contact with strangers in big cities than in small towns. People would be less likely to make eye contact in bus stations, for example, than in more
15 comfortable settings such as a university student center.
[N]   Patterns of eye contact are different across cultures. Some Americans feel uncomfortable with the °"gaze" that is sometimes

associated with Arab or Indian communication patterns. For Americans, this style of eye contact is too intense. Yet too little eye
5 contact may also be viewed negatively, because it may convey a lack of interest, inattention, or even °mistrust. The relationship between the lack of eye contact and mistrust in the American culture is stated directly in the expression, "Never trust a person who doesn't look you in the eyes." In contrast, in many other parts of the world (espe-
10 cially in Asian countries), a person's lack of eye contact toward an authority figure °signifies respect and °deference.

Conversational Distance

[O] °Unconsciously, we all keep a comfortable distance around us when we interact with other people. This distance has had several names over the years, including "personal space," "interpersonal distance," "comfort zone," and °"body bubble." This space between us and
5 another person forms °invisible walls that define how comfortable we feel at various distances from other people.

[P]   The amount of space changes depending on the °nature of the relationship. For example, we are usually more comfortable standing closer to family members than to strangers. Personality also determines the size of the area with which we are comfortable when talk-
5 ing to people. °Introverts often prefer to interact with others at a

greater distance than do °extroverts. Cultural styles are important too. A Japanese employer and employee usually stand farther apart while talking than their American °counterparts. Latin Americans and Arabs tend to stand closer than Americans do when talking.

[Q]   For Americans, the usual distance in social conversation ranges from about an arm's length to four feet. Less space in the American culture may be °associated with either greater intimacy or °aggressive behavior.[4] The common practice of saying, "Excuse me," for the

5   slightest °accidental touching of another person reveals how uncomfortable Americans are if people get too close. Thus, a person whose "space" has been °intruded upon by another may feel °threatened and

react °defensively. In cultures where close physical contact is acceptable and even desirable, Americans may be perceived as cold and
10   distant.

[R]   Culture does not always determine the message of nonverbal
communication. The individual's personality, the context, and the
relationship also influence its meaning. However, like verbal language, nonverbal language is °linked to a person's cultural back-
5   ground. People are generally comfortable with others who have
"body language" similar to their own. One research study demonstrated that when British graduate students imitated some Arab patterns of nonverbal behavior (making increased eye contact, smiling,
and directly facing their Arab partners), the Arabs felt that these stu-
10   dents were more likeable and trustworthy than most of the other
British students.[5]

[S]   When one person's nonverbal language °matches that of another,
there is increased comfort. In nonverbal communication across cultures there are similarities and differences. Whether we choose to
emphasize the former or the latter, the "silent language" is much
5   louder than it first appears.

Comprehension Questions*

Note that this section now contains multiple-choice and open-ended
questions.

1. The quotations at the beginning of the reading are examples of
   how people can misinterpret:
   (a) nonverbal communication.
   b. verbal communication.
   c. cultural values.

2. Many people think that it is the spoken word that is most important in conversation. This perception is often: [A]
   a. true.
   (b.) not true.
   c. exact.

3. According to the authors, when do people express themselves
   more verbally than nonverbally?   [B, C]

4. The authors say that nonverbal communication expresses meaning or feeling: [D]

*The capital letters in brackets refer to the corresponding paragraphs in the reading.

a. with many words.

b. with song and dance.

c. with no words.

5. According to the authors, feelings of friendship are universal, but their expression is: [E]

a. not always the same.

b. usually exactly the same.

c. not very different.

6. The authors state that if people want to understand other cultural styles of communication, they should study the "silent language" of that culture. Of what four aspects of nonverbal communication do the authors say people are not usually aware? [F]

7. The authors tell us that hand movements can convey meaning. Are the meanings of gestures the same in all cultures? Give some examples of differences. [G]

8. According to the authors, when do people imitate and learn their nonverbal communication? [H]

9. The authors say that the meaning of facial expressions is determined by: [J]

a. relationships.

b. situations.

c. feelings.

d. both (a) and (b).

10. According to the authors, facial expressions show emotions and attitudes. Can you assume that people from other cultures know the exact meaning of your facial expressions? Give an example of a situation in which there might be cross-cultural misinterpretations. [K]

11. The fact that members of one culture don't express their emotions as openly as members of another means that: [K]

a. they do not experience emotions as intensely as others do.

b. cultural rules affect how expressive a person can be.

c. cultural rules forbid any nonverbal expressiveness in some cultures.

12. Eye contact is important because too much or too little eye contact can create: [M]

a. communications barriers.

b. interesting relationships.

c. strange expressions.

13. According to the authors, what determines the comfortable distance when we interact with other people?   [P]

a. the nature of the relationship

b. personalities

c. cultural styles

d. all of the above

14. The authors say that in cultures where close physical contact is important, Americans are sometimes perceived as: [Q]

a. distant and cold.

b. cold and close.

c. quiet and distant.

15. The authors say that when the nonverbal language of one person matches the nonverbal language of another person, there is: [S]

a. increased discomfort.

b. decreased comfort.

c. increased comfort.

Discussion Questions

Students should prepare these before class discussion.

1. In Paragraph A, the authors discuss how people can misinterpret nonverbal language that is culturally different from their own. Has this ever happened to you? Describe what took place and your reactions to the incident.

2. In Paragraph C, the authors describe a study that found that 93 percent of a person's attitude was communicated nonverbally and only 7 percent with words. If this study were done in your country, do you think the results would be the same? Explain your answer.

3. The authors discuss the expression of emotion in Paragraph D. Do people from your culture show their happiness and sadness openly? What cross-cultural similarities and differences in the area of facial expressiveness have you observed?

4. Do you think it is important to understand other cultural communication styles? Explain your answer. In Paragraph F, what do

the authors suggest that people do to understand other cultural styles of communication better?   [F]

5. In Paragraph H, the authors tell us that not all gestures are universal. What gestures do you know of that have the same meaning in more than one culture? What gestures have different meanings across cultures?

6. In Paragraph J, the authors tell us that Americans smile at strangers, although this is not so common in big cities. Why do you think this is true? What is your experience?

7. What explanation for an American teacher's difficulty in a Japanese classroom do the authors suggest in Paragraph K? What advice would you give a new American teacher in Japan?

8. According to the authors' statements in Paragraph L, should people judge others according to their own cultural norms? Do you agree? Why or why not?

9. What is the American expression about eye contact that is quoted in Paragraph N? Why is it not a universal belief?

10. In Paragraph O, the authors describe conversational distance as the space that forms "invisible walls" around a person. If someone is standing too close to you (because of that person's cultural practice), what would you do or say? Would you inform that person? Would you use verbal or nonverbal communication? Explain your answer.

Vocabulary Exercises

Vocabulary List

As you read the vocabulary list below, find two or three words you already know. Give their definitions.

Paragraph A	*Paragraph B*	*Paragraph C*
misinterpret	emphasized	transmitted
nonverbal	withdrawal _retrada_	
communication	convey	

Paragraph D	*Paragraph E*	*Paragraph F*
universal	affection	determine
mourn _lamentar_		
subdued _dominar_		

Paragraph G	*Paragraph H*	*Paragraph I*
gestures	imitate	distributed
beckoning hablar q/señales	accompany	
	obscene	

Paragraph J	*Paragraph K*	*Paragraph M*
disguise disfrazar	expressiveness	insufficient
suspicious	exhibits	excessive
	responsiveness	intimacy
		glance echar un vistazo
		presence

Paragraph N	*Paragraph O*	*Paragraph P*
gaze mirar	unconsciously	nature
mistrust desconfianza	body bubble	introverts
signifies	invisible	extroverts
deference		counterparts duplicado

Paragraph Q	*Paragraph R*	*Paragraph S*
associated	linked conectar	matches
aggressive		
accidental		
intruded intruso, estorbar		
threatened amenazar		
defensively		

A. Definitions

Choose the correct word for the definition from the list below. Then fill in the blanks in the sentences following the definitions. *Note: You may have to change the grammatical form of the word used in the sentence.*

glance [M]	intruded [Q]
introverts [P]	threatened [Q]
extroverts [P]	associated [Q]
counterparts [P]	accidental [Q]
invisible [O]	matches [S]
defensively [Q]	

1. Definition: expressed an intention of hurting or punishing

   threaten

   The teacher's threaten didn't mean anything; he never followed through with them.

2. Definition: shy, inward people ___introverts___

   The ___introvert___ young woman was not hired by the public relations firm; she instead got a job in a bookstore.

3. Definition: connected ___associated___

   The retired professor was ___associated___ with the University of Ulm for twenty years.

4. Definition: forced oneself on others without being asked or welcomed ___intruded___

   The ___intruded___ sensed that he was not wanted at the party.

5. Definition: happening by chance; not on purpose ___accidentaly___

   The car ___accidentaly___ hit the tree.

6. Definition: bold, outward people ___extroverts___

   Do you have to be a ___extrovert___ to be an actor?

7. Definition: unable to be seen ___invisible___

   Most people think that ghosts are ___invisibles___.

8. Definition: people or things that correspond to others in form and function; equivalents ___counterparts___

   The assistant director of the company felt that his ___counterparts___ in the other offices were not doing their jobs well.

9. Definition: in a manner of feeling attacked and justifying quickly.

   ___defensive___

   It can be difficult to talk with people who are ___defensive___.

10. Definition: corresponds with ___match___

    Your shoes ___matches___ your trousers, but they don't ___match___ your shirt.

11. Definition: to look at briefly ___glance___

    She ___glance___ at the beautiful tree and continued her afternoon jog.

B. Synonyms

Choose the appropriate synonym from the list to replace the italicized word, and rewrite each sentence. *Change tense, singular and plural usage, and part of speech when necessary.*

5 love   10 connected
1 stressed   6 call ed
2 backing away 7 copy ing
3 send   9 indecent
4 global   8 go with

1. The student *emphasized* his ideas by speaking more loudly. [B]

   The student stressed his ideas by speaking more loudly

2. Her *withdrawal* from the group showed her dislike of its members. [B]

   Her backing away from the group showed her dislike of its members.

3. The message was *transmitted* by radio. [C]

   The message was sended by radio

4. Handshaking is not a *universal* gesture in introductions. [D]

   Handshaking is not a global gesture in introductions

5. *Affection* can be shown emotionally and physically. [E]

   Love can be shown emotionally and physically

6. I *beckoned* the waiter to come to our table. [G]

   I called the waiter to come to our table

7. Children learn gestures by *imitating* their parents' movements. [H]

   Children learn gestures by copying their parent's movements.

8. Did you *accompany* your younger brother to the movie last night? [H]

   Did you go with your younger brother to the movie last night?

9. The exhibit was closed because some of the photographs were said to be *obscene*. [H]

   The exhibit was closed because some of the photographs were said to be indecent

10. After years of research, smoking was *linked* to birth defects. [R]

    After years of research, smoking was connected with birth defects.

C. Matching

Match the words with their definitions. Place the letter of the definition in the space next to the word.

_j_ body bubble

_m_ convey

_b_ nonverbal communication

_d_ mourn

_l_ responsiveness

_h_ deference

_a_ gestures

_e_ distributed

_f_ presence

_g_ gaze

_c_ misinterpret

_i_ unconsciously

_k_ facial expressiveness

a. movements of the body or part of the body, especially the hands

b. communication that is "silent," and includes the use of gestures, facial expressions, eye contact, and conversation distance

c. not understand correctly

d. feel or express sorrow

e. spread; delivered

f. existence

g. fixed, intent stare

h. formal respect

i. without knowing; not purposefully

j. the personal space that surrounds an individual

k. demonstration of emotion or feeling visible on the face

l. degree of reaction

m. communicate; send

D. Multiple Choice

Choose the word that *best* defines the italicized word.

1. Children tend to be loud when they play, whereas adults are more *subdued*.   [D]

   a. quiet

   b. active

   c. patient

   d. sleepy

2. The sad child tried to *disguise* her feelings by smiling.   [J]

   a. discover

   b. expose

   c. hide

   d. resist

3. The man left the store without buying anything and the owner thought his behavior was *suspicious*.   [J]
   a. questionable   c. mean
   b. rude   d. poor

4. My sister *exhibits* such rude behavior that no one wants to be her friend.   [K]
   a. displays   c. becomes
   b. announces   d. wants

5. *Insufficient* knowledge of his job caused him many problems at work.   [M]
   a. not enough   c. inappropriate
   b. incorrect   d. too much

6. *Excessive* spending may result in poverty.   [M]
   a. thrifty   c. careful
   b. exclusive   d. extravagant

7. It takes time to build emotional *intimacy*.   [M]
   a. privacy   c. expression
   b. closeness   d. sanity

8. She showed her *mistrust* of doctors by ignoring her doctor's advice.   [N]
   a. disdain desdeñoso   c. lack of loyalty
   b. disease enfermedad   d. lack of trust

9. A gesture in one country often *signifies* a different message in another country.   [N]
   a. means   c. shows
   b. says   d. argues

10. The *nature* of their conversation was professional.   [P]
    a. type   c. category
    b. outdoors   d. talk

11. The lion became *aggressive* when he was hungry.   [Q]
    a. tired   c. hostile
    b. sad   d. moody raro, deprimido

Conversational Activities

A. Gestures

The following are some of the more common gestures used in American culture. These are movements that are made with hands, arms, and shoulders; each has a specific meaning. Demonstrate them in class, and discuss any cross-cultural differences in their meaning.

Ask your teacher to demonstrate typical American gestures that convey boredom, excessive talking, and money.

O.K.

Good luck. I hope it works out.

Don't ask me; I don't know.

I didn't hear you.
I can't hear you.

Cut; that's enough.
Stop, or it's all over for me.

Oh, I forgot!
Don't tell me [surprised]!

Wait a second.
Slow down.
Relax.

Come here.

Act out the following situations, practicing the gestures listed above and those demonstrated by your teacher.

You can't hear your friend's voice.

You want a child to come to your side.

Your friend has just walked into the class to take an important examination. Wish him or her good luck.

Somebody has asked you a question, and you don't know the answer.

You want to tell your friend that the lecture is boring.

You signal to your friend that the person on the phone is talking too much.

You are ready to enter the restaurant when you notice that a simple dinner costs almost $25.

B. Eye Contact

In pairs, carry on conversations using different types of eye contact: (1) minimal eye contact; (2) gazing; and (3) your natural style of eye contact.

Discuss

1. Did the variations in eye contact affect your conversation?

2. Have you had any experiences where people have used different types of eye contact? Discuss.

C. Charades

Pantomime ideas and emotions to the rest of the class. Think of sentences or phrases to illustrate nonverbally. For example:

I'm mad!

This is delicious!

Your baby is beautiful!

Please leave.

Write down your ideas, feelings, and expressions, and give them to other class members to act out, or act them out yourself. Do not use any words. See if the other class members can guess the meanings.

D. Nonverbal Cues

Nonverbal cues or behavior can carry negative meaning in certain situations and positive meaning in others. For instance, when a father stares at his son who has just failed an exam, that stare conveys something negative. However, when a painter stares at a model who is about to be painted, that stare does not have a negative meaning. In this exercise, indicate whether you feel the nonverbal cues listed are negative or positive. There are four possible relationships given for each one.

Directions: In the chart on p. 123, place a (+) in the blanks in which the nonverbal cue is positive and a (−) in the blanks in which the cue is negative. Place a (+) and a (−) if you feel that the cue can be either.

Discuss

1. Compare your responses with those of the other class members. Were any cues positive in one situation and negative in another?

2. Were any neutral?

3. Did you disagree with the other class members? If so, why?

E. Role-Playing

Working in pairs (with two people from the same culture if possible),* write a dialogue *in your own language* and *then in English* using the following situation. First perform the dialogue in front of the class in your own language. Then perform the same scene in English. The class members will comment on the nonverbal behavior they observe in both scenes.

---

*If class members are from one culture, role-play different situations (e.g., meeting a friend at a party, making a date, or returning a bad product to a store manager).

A student is entering a professor's office to discuss a problem. After a short conversation, the student leaves the office. (Demonstrate how the student enters the office, greets the professor, discusses the problem, and leaves.)

Discuss

1. Did you feel or observe any nonverbal differences when you switched languages?
2. Were you more comfortable in one language than in another?
3. Do your body movements change when you are speaking a foreign language? If so, how?

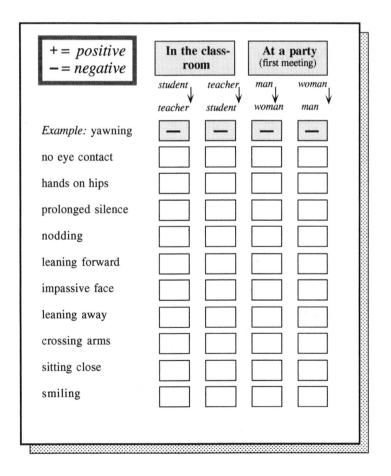

+ = *positive* − = *negative*	In the class- room		At a party (first meeting)	
	student ↓ *teacher*	*teacher* ↓ *student*	*man* ↓ *woman*	*woman* ↓ *man*
Example: yawning	−	−	−	−
no eye contact				
hands on hips				
prolonged silence				
nodding				
leaning forward				
impassive face				
leaning away				
crossing arms				
sitting close				
smiling				

F. Observation Task

The purpose of this activity is to develop observational skills and to discuss nonverbal communication.

Directions: Working in pairs or in groups of three or four, observe people's use of space, eye contact, touching, and gestures; suggested areas for your observations are listed below. Record your observations in the spaces provided. After the observation, meet with class members and discuss the follow-up questions.

Suggested Areas for Making Observations

✓restaurants	coffee shops
outdoor seating areas	book store
bus stops	classrooms
library	elevators

1. Use of space
   a. During greetings and farewells
      Between 8 men and women they had a short distance in their farewells and she just say "by-bye".
   b. Between men and women (sitting and standing) shaking her hand
      They are very close and sometimes he touchs her hand on the table, so maybe the're a good friends or a couple.
   c. Between members of the same sex (sitting and standing)
      They have more distance than men and women.
      They're talking very loud and loughing
   d. Between friends
      Their space is really short. They're eating on a table and they're very close.
   e. Between strangers
      They don't know each other so they've a huge distance.
2. Eye contact and touching
   a. During greetings and farewells
      Most of the people say 'Hello' and 'God-bye' whit a kiss, or, shaking their hand or touching the arm or the shou-
   b. Between men and women engaged in conversations lder of the other person.
      They see each other deeply and slowly
      'cause I supose they know.
   c. Between members of the same sex
      Sometimes she is looking at her, and others she does not.

d. Between strangers approaching each other (specifically eye contact)

When one of them find the looking of the other person, they just say "Hi, How are you doing !?" and that's all.

3. Gestures (hand and facial)

a. During greetings and farewells

When they met each other they had a smile in their face. Others, had a hug or shake hands

b. Between men and women

He's looking at her very deep, paying attention and listening every word that she says.

c. Between members of the same sex

They are laughing, paying attention and following his conversation with facial gestures and eye contact.

d. Between strangers

They don't expresse a lot of cheer and enthusiasm when they met or see each other.

Follow-up

1. How close to each other did people stand or sit?

2. How much touching took place?

3. What did you notice about eye behavior?

4. What gestures did people use?

5. Could you tell when a conversation was going to end? If so, how?

6. What were the feelings between two people talking? How did each show interest in the other person?

7. Could you interpret the social relationships between two people talking (e.g., close friends, students, teacher-student, boyfriend-girlfriend)?

G. Nonverbal Communication: Description and Opinion

There are several ways of making observations. One way is simply to describe what you see. Another way is to give an opinion or make a judgment about your observation. For example:

Men do not maintain frequent eye contact with each other. (*Description*)

Men do not seem to feel close to each other. (*Opinion*)

Directions: After each of the following statements, check either *description* or *opinion*, depending on the type of observation made.

	Description	Opinion
1. The woman was aggressive because she stood close to the man.		✓
2. The two men embraced each other two times before leaving.	✓	
3. The woman stood three feet from the man.	✓	
4. They are superficial because they smile at each other even though they are strangers.		✓
5. Their farewell was cold because they didn't touch each other.		✓
6. The two women walked arm-in-arm for an hour.	✓	
7. Because fathers and sons do not hug, they do not love each other.		✓
8. The teacher did not stand near the children.	✓	

Discuss

1. In the "Observation Task" activity above, were your observations descriptive or judgmental (i.e., based on opinion)?
2. What is the problem with making opinionated or judgmental observations in a foreign culture?
3. Is it possible to make purely descriptive observations?

H. Multiple-Choice Questionnaire

The following questions are intended to stimulate cross-cultural discussion and to help you become familiar with American customs and responses. First, write an answer that describes a likely response in your country. On the multiple-choice questions, try to guess what an American would do. *More than one answer may be correct.*

1. Signaling a waiter is done by:

   In your country: _____

In the United States:

a. Snapping the fingers.

b. Whistling.

c. Raising one hand briefly.

d. Saying, "Waiter," and gesturing to him.

2. How do people end conversations nonverbally?

   In your country: _____

   In the United States:

   a. They look at their watches.

   b. They look away from the speaker.

   c. They back up slowly.

   d. They stop talking abruptly.

3. The best way to get a teacher's attention is to:

   In your country: _____

   In the United States:

   a. Snap your fingers.

   b. Raise your hand until the teacher calls on you.

   c. Raise your hand and lower it when the teacher notices that you have a question.

   d. Call out the teacher's name.

4. When you are being introduced, what do you do in addition to speaking (e.g., what do you do with your hands)?

   In your country: _____

   In the United States:

   a. Shake hands lightly.

   b. Shake hands firmly for a few seconds.

   c. Shake hands until the introduction is completely finished.

   d. Shake hands and then bow.

5. When you are being introduced, what kind of eye contact do you use?

   In your country: _____

   In the United States:

   a. Make direct eye contact.

   b. Avoid eye contact.

   c. Make eye contact and then quickly look away.

   d. Make eye contact and then look at the floor.

6. Nonverbally, how would you get the attention of a busy secretary in an office?

In your country: _____

In the United States:

   a. Stand by the door and wait until the secretary looks at you.

   b. Stand close to the secretary until you are noticed.

   c. Sit down near the secretary and remain silent until you are noticed.

   d. Tap the secretary on the shoulder.

7. If a student does not understand a point that a teacher makes in class, it is best to:

In your country: _____

In the United States:

   a. Raise a hand and ask for clarification.

   b. Look confused.

   c. Remain silent and ask the teacher after class.

   d. Leave the class.

8. How do you motion to a person to come to you?

In your country: _____

In the United States:

   a. Extend both arms in front of you and, with your palms up, wave to the person to come.

   b. Roll your eyes in the direction you want the person to come.

   c. Extend one arm in front of you and, with your palm up, wave to the person to come.

   d. Extend one arm in front of you and, with your palm down, wave to the person to come.

I. Cross-Cultural Questions

Answer the following questions about your own culture, and then discuss cross-cultural similarities and differences.

1. Do you recall from your childhood how you learned aspects of nonverbal language (space, gestures, etc.)?

2. Are there any expressions or proverbs in your language that say something about nonverbal communication? For example, in English there is the expression, "He shakes hands like a dead fish."

3. What kind of impressions do people form of one another based on nonverbal behavior (e.g., "I don't trust him because he stares at people.")?

4. What should a foreigner learn about nonverbal communication in your country before going there?

Cultural Notes

1. Because the United States is a nation of many minority groups (African-Americans, Mexicans, Chinese, Italians, Jews, Japanese, Koreans, Arabs, Vietnamese, etc.), it is difficult to make generalizations about American nonverbal communication. For example, touching behavior among Mexican-Americans differs from that among Anglo-Americans. For the Anglo-American, touching is more restricted. The Anglo-American male rarely touches or embraces other males. Distance is usually greater between men in the Anglo-American culture than between men in the Mexican-American culture.

2. Edward Hall, in his book *The Hidden Dimension*, discusses four categories of informal use of space among white, professional-class Americans:[6]

For intimate friends	From actual physical contact to 18 inches
For friends and personal conversation	18 inches to 4 feet
For impersonal conversation	4 feet to 12 feet
For public speaking	12 feet or more

3. Americans believe that a firm and brief handshake is a sign of confidence, whereas a loose handshake signifies a lack of character or strength.

4. During the farewell stage of a conversation, Americans will often move gradually away from each other and decrease eye contact. This, of course, is not a rule but it does happen. Consider the following sample dialogue:

Brian: "It was nice meeting you." (1 foot apart)

Betsy: "Hope to see you again sometime." (6 feet apart)

Brian: "Take care." (15 feet apart)

Supplementary Vocabulary

to move	to whistle	to retreat
to make contact	to mumble	to withdraw
to back away	to recline	attraction
to yawn	to advance	posture
to sigh		

5

Relationships: Friends and Acquaintances

"Everyone's friend is no one's friend."

Italian Proverb

"Cooked at one stirring makes friends too easily."

Chinese Proverb

"Friends are made in wine and proven in tears."

German Proverb

"When husband and wife agree, they will be able to dry up the oceans with buckets."

Vietnamese Proverb

"To those we love best, we say the least."

Filipino Proverb

Pre-Reading Discussion

1. Discuss the meaning of the proverbs on friendship. Some of the sayings are universal; some of them may not be. Which ones do you think are true in all cultures?

2. Do you have any impressions of American friendships? Do you think there are cultural differences in the way people make and keep friends? Explain.

3. How do people meet people of the same sex in your country? How do they meet people of the opposite sex?

4. Do people in your country tend to live in one place or move around? Do you stay in touch with friends even if they move away?

5. What do you expect of a close friend? What do you expect of a casual friend? Have you ever had an experience with an American or someone else from another culture where each of you had different expectations of the friendship?

Pre-Reading Vocabulary

1. Definitions

   a. **friendliness**: behavior, characterized by smiling, chattiness, and warmth, that demonstrates interest in another person (adjective = "friendly")

   b. **friendship**: a relationship in which people know, like, and trust each other

   Discussion: In your country, if someone is friendly, does that mean the person wants to become your friend? In your country, is it acceptable or usual to be friendly to strangers? Explain.

2. Definition

   "**singles scene**": the situation of single people; usually used to describe what single people do to meet other people

   Discussion: How do single people meet others in your country? Are they introduced? Do they meet because they have similar interests? How did your parents meet? What do you think Americans do to meet people?

3. Definitions

   a. **transient**: short-term; temporary

   b. **permanent**: long-term; lasting

Discussion: In your country, do people have transient friendships as well as permanent ones? When you make friends, are they your friends "for life"? Some foreigners have a stereotyped belief that many Americans have shallow and transient friendships. Do you agree with the stereotype? Why or why not?

Skimming: For General Information

To get the general idea of the reading that follows:

1. Read the titles and headings of the sections.
2. Read the first and last paragraphs of the reading.

From your skimming, answer the following:

1. For Americans, does the word "friend" refer to one type or a variety of types of personal relationships?

Scanning: For Specific Information

To find specific information in the reading, look for clues such as certain words and numbers. Scan the reading to find the answers to the following:

1. Approximately how many Americans relocate every year? Why do they move? Where did you find your answer?
2. The authors mention that some languages have different translations of the word "privacy." What three languages do they use as examples? What is the translation of "privacy" in these languages?

Reading Text

Relationships: Friends and Acquaintances

"Friend"   Close childhood friend
"Friend"   Best friend
"Friend"   New friend
"Friend"   Family friend
"Friend"   Classmate
"Friend"   Teammate

"Friend"	Colleague or co-worker
"Friend"	Roommate or housemate
"Friend"	Girlfriend or boyfriend
"Friend"	Acquaintance

[A] What do Americans mean when they use the word "friend"? The dictionary defines it as: "one attached to another by affection or esteem." Americans, however, use the word more freely than the dictionary definition. A friend might be an °acquaintance or an intimate companion that one has known since childhood. It is difficult to define this word °precisely as it is used in American English, because it covers many different relationships. "My friend and I took our kids to the park yesterday." "My friend told me about a wonderful restaurant." "My friend listened to my problems for two hours yesterday." We hear such daily uses of the word "friend" without knowing the quality of the friendship mentioned.

[B]   In general, Americans have °casual, friendly relationships with many people, but deeper, closer friendships with only a few. True friendships require time and °commitment, which many Americans lack. Therefore, they often find it convenient to have friendly but less committed relationships, rather than many deep, close friendships. Unlike the stereotype, Americans do indeed have close friends, but in

addition they have friendships that can be characterized as °superfi-
cial. Their shortage of time and their numerous commitments to family, work, and even volunteer projects mean Americans have less time
10 to °pursue many close friends.

°Friendliness Versus °Friendship

[C] Many people around the world characterize Americans as friendly.
Americans, especially in comparison to certain other cultural groups,
tend to smile and talk easily with others even if they are strangers (in
big cities, this is less common). For example, people waiting in lines
5 (i.e., in the post office or in the grocery store) often °strike up conversations with each other. They may even °disclose personal information in °encounters with strangers whom they will never see again.
This seems unusual to many foreigners in the United States. From
their point of view, how can a person trust a stranger enough to chat
10 freely and reveal personal information? After all, in most of the
world, strangers are not to be trusted.
[D]   The following is an account of what an American woman
learned about the American man she was standing behind in a line in
a post office. In about eight minutes, he °revealed that: (1) he was
married and his wife was about to have a baby; (2) he was unhappy
5 with his job as a salesman and was considering a "mid-life" career
change (not uncommon in the United States); (3) he and his wife
were trying to figure out if it would be better to work harder or to
take more time off from work so that they could relax more.
[E]   This is perhaps an extreme example (even for many Americans)
of how strangers reveal aspects of their lives to each other. To many
people around the world, this openness would be considered abnor-
mal and even suspicious. Some would stereotype this man and might
5 say, "Well, he's a salesman. What do you expect?" While many
Americans would find his openness excessive, this type of person is
not a °rarity.

Diversity in Personal Relationships

[F] In the United States, men and women °socialize relatively freely and
develop a variety of relationships. To people from cultures where
contact between the sexes is °limited (or even forbidden), this variety
can be confusing. Single and married people of the opposite sex may
5 be close friends and share personal problems without being romanti-
cally involved. College students and others may even live with someone of the opposite sex for °practical reasons only. That is, they may
be friends (without any romantic connection) who feel that they are

°compatible as "roommates" or "housemates." In contrast, many men
10 and women decide to live together before they are married to see how
compatible they are. Some of these relationships end up in successful
marriages; others break up before (and some after) marriage. In many
parts of the United States (although not all), there are few restrictions
15 on the types of relationships people can have. This does not mean
that you will see nontraditional relationships everywhere you go in
the United States. However, in some of the big cities and in areas not
characterized as "conservative," you will see a great deal of variety in
types of personal relationships.

[G]   In the United States, marriage relationships, of course, differ
from couple to couple, but there are some generalities that can be
made. Some married men and women consider themselves to be best
friends as well as spouses. This concept is unusual in some cultures,
5 particularly where the marriage is °arranged or is a marriage of convenience. Some foreigners in the United States have mentioned that it
is impossible for a spouse to be a best friend. On the other hand,
some Americans hold the same belief, but probably not for cultural
reasons.

[H]   Many people remarry if they have been divorced or widowed.
Remarriage has no °stigma in the United States. In fact, some widowed or divorced people are encouraged by their grown children to
continue to socialize and even remarry. Indeed, many older people
5   feel that they have a right to continued happiness in personal relationships regardless of their age. Therefore, more people have been
seeking companionships with new friends in their °"golden years."

The "Singles Scene"

[I]   Recently, there has been a dramatic rise in the number of single people in the United States, in part due to the large number of "baby
boomers" (people born between 1945 and 1960). The increase is also
due to people delaying marriage until their late twenties. Further-
5   more, because many women now have a higher educational and economic status than before, they do not feel that they need the financial
security traditionally associated with marriage. As a result, marriage
is viewed by some more as a choice rather than a °necessity.
Although marriage is still an extremely important social institution in
10   this country, there is less pressure to marry at a young age and, in
some cases, to marry at all.

[J] Changing American norms about marriage sometimes strike people from more traditional cultures as unusual. Unmarried Americans have been asked such questions as, "When are you going to get married?" or "Why aren't you married?" In general, these questions are

5 too direct and too personal, even for Americans. An American can be offended by these questions, even though for the foreigner or newcomer in the United States, the questions are °innocent and friendly. Once again, because of the value Americans place on individualism, many Americans do not want to feel that they have to conform to

10 societal expectations (e.g., getting married at a particular age).

[K] How do singles meet each other in the United States? °Mutual friends, parties, work, religious groups, and various dating services account for many of the ways that singles meet. Generally the "bar scene," although a popular place to socialize, is not considered an

5 ideal setting to meet romantic °partners. At a bar, most encounters are °random; people do not meet each other because they share an interest. The stigma of a "pick-up" also makes some women and men hesitant to choose bars as a respectable place to meet people of the opposite sex.

[L] °Social networks, including family, friends, and even acquaintances, are more likely to offer opportunities to meet new people. Within recent years, there has been an escalation in the number of dating services that assist singles in meeting new people with similar

5 backgrounds. These services include personal advertisements in magazines and newspapers. Other dating services utilize videos and computers. Usually, they charge a fee, and some can be quite °exorbitant.

Mobility and Friendship

[M] Americans are geographically °mobile, and many learn to develop friendships easily and quickly. Approximately one out of every five American families moves every year.[1] People °relocate because they change jobs, attend distant colleges, get married, have children, or

5 simply want a change in their lives. Perhaps as a consequence, people sometimes form and end friendships quickly. Students who attend two or three universities during their undergraduate and graduate years may change their "circle of friends" several times. Likewise, people who change their jobs, while keeping one or two

10 friends from the original place of employment, may also change their circle of friends.

[N] Relationships based on a common activity may °fade or end when the activity ends. Mothers may meet while dropping their children off at nursery school and remain friends until their kids go to different schools. The same holds true for neighbors who are closest

5 of friends until one moves away. These friendships are not deep but are based upon shared daily experiences. Many Americans, in general, do have °enduring friendships, but at certain points in their lives can be satisfied with °transient relationships. In cultures where people have only lifetime friends (in part because they do not move from

10 city to city), these temporary relationships are hard to understand. But many Americans move so often that learning to make friends quickly becomes a necessary survival skill.

Cross-Cultural Friendships

[O] One of the most frequent problems in cross-cultural relationships is that foreigners misinterpret American friendliness as an offer of friendship. Naturally, a foreigner who thinks that an American is °extending friendship would have expectations for the friendship.

5 When the American is unaware of these expectations or is unwilling to be a true friend (because all that was °intended was a friendly but superficial relationship), the foreigner or newcomer in the United States can become disappointed.

[P]   On the surface, when Americans are being friendly, it may seem that they are °initiating a friendship. It is useful for foreign students, visitors, and immigrants to know that Americans can actually be shy in interactions with foreigners. This is partly due to the Americans'
5   linguistic and geographic isolation, especially in parts of the United States without diverse populations. In general, it is advisable to approach Americans first to initiate friendships. Some Americans will want to go beyond a superficial friendship, depending on whether they have the time to make the commitment. One foreign
10   student, having lived in the United States for several years, said that the most important advice he could give to newcomers would be: "Don't be passive when it comes to making friends with Americans. Begin conversations, extend invitations, and make the first move."

Cross-Cultural Expectations for Friendship

[Q]   Expectations for personal relationships differ greatly across cultures. It is important to know that while most Americans value close friend-ships, they also value privacy and independence. From an American

perspective, to have privacy or to give someone privacy is considered
5   positive. Yet, when the word "privacy" is translated into other languages (e.g., Russian, Arabic, and Japanese), it has more of a negative
meaning. (In these languages "privacy" means aloneness or loneliness.) Therefore, the American's need for privacy is sometimes
judged negatively by those who have not been raised with the value
10 of individualism. Some Americans are isolated from others because
they have taken their independence and privacy to an extreme.
Others simply like spending time alone or at least having the freedom
to °avoid socializing if they choose. An Argentinian explained to his
American co-workers that in Argentina he felt pressured to go out
15 with his friends on Friday and Saturday nights. In the United States,
he felt that if he chose to have a quiet evening at home, no one would
ask him, "Why?" Although he missed his friends from his country,
he appreciated the freedom to have more privacy in the United
States.

[R]   In any true friendship, whatever the culture may be, a person is
expected to show interest and concern in a friend's serious problems.
But how does one show this across cultures? It is not possible to generalize about Americans because there are so many varieties of
5   Americans, but it is possible to say that many foreigners or newcomers from different cultures have felt disappointed by Americans. A
common °occurrence is when an American does not phone or visit as

much as the foreigner expects. If someone from another culture is
having a serious problem, Americans may say, "Let me know if
10 there's anything I can do to help." If the Americans do not receive a
specific request, they may feel that there's nothing they can do. In
this case, they may call every now and then to stay in touch. The
friend from a different culture, on the other hand, may be expecting
°"sympathy calls" or frequent visits, and may not hesitate to demon-
15 strate a dependence on a friend. For example, an American woman
reported that a friend from the Middle East who was living in the
United States called her every day when she only had a cold. Many
Americans are uncomfortable when people become too dependent.

[S]   In addition, an American may feel that a friend needs privacy to
°"work out" a problem. Many Americans want such time alone when
they have problems. So an American may want to give you your pri-

vacy even if you don't want it! In some cultures, it may be the case
5   that a friend would spend as much time as possible with someone
having a serious problem. It is hard to generalize on this point, but
some Americans may feel that they are °"bothering" people in such a
circumstance. Of course, the time friends spend with each other
varies depending on the nature of the problem and the type of friend-
10 ship.

[T]   In addition to different expectations about the amount of time
spent together, there are also cultural differences in what people
believe they should do for each other. An American's friendship with
a Russian immigrant broke up because the American was asked to do
5   something above and beyond what the person would normally do for
an American friend. The person from Russia asked the American to
co-sign a loan; in other words, the American's signature would indicate a °willingness to pay back a loan to a bank if the Russian immigrant was not able to do so. The American, with his sense of °finan-
10 cial responsibility to his family, felt that the favor asked was
excessive, even though he was almost sure that his Russian friend
would be able to °repay the loan. The Russian, who felt very close to
the American, did not see this as an unreasonable request. The
American ended up telling the Russian that, although he would very
15 much like to help him, he would not co-sign the loan. After that, the
Russian never called him, and when the American called him, the
wife said, "He's busy now." Neither person did anything intentional-
ly to end the friendship; in fact, both felt bad about what had happened.

[U]   The problem between these two men was that their °expecta-
tions about friendship differed. In this case, the American was
expected to help solve a day-to-day problem that, from the
American's standpoint, should have been solved by an agency or
5   organization. From the Russian immigrant's °perspective, which was
shaped by his experiences in his country, friends, by necessity,
become each other's "social service agencies." It is important to realize that if an American °behaves differently from what you expect in
a personal relationship, do not assume that the friendship is over or
10 that the person is not a true friend.

Benefits of Cross-Cultural Contact

[V]   Necessary ingredients for a true friendship consist of shared experiences, values, and interests. Across cultures, shared daily experience
does not exist, but through initial superficial relationships people can
discover whether they have shared values and interests. Even if a
5   relationship is superficial or "does not go anywhere," the cross-cultural contact can still be °beneficial to both parties and can help

break down isolation and stereotypes. The most °obvious benefit to the language learner is the opportunity for language practice. In addition, the more experience people have in initiating and responding to
10 relationships, whether transient or °permanent, superficial or deep, the more clues they will have to understanding the deep culture in which they live.

[W]   Without the experience of encountering people in several types of relationships, it is difficult to learn to become comfortable in the second culture. There is no doubt that engaging in personal relationships across cultures requires more time and effort, and can be more
5 tiring than doing so with people from one's own culture.

[X]   There are benefits to socializing with people from the same culture. When people have contact with those similar in background, culture shock can be lessened. It is important to have this familiarity when everything else is different. In addition, individuals can truly
5 relax and be themselves when they are with others who share a common culture and language. However, socializing *only* with those from the same country is not as desirable as having the additional cross-cultural contact. Being involved in relationships across cultures will °assist in °acculturation and, °ultimately, integration into the new
10 society.

Comprehension Questions*

1. The authors say that Americans use the word "friend" differently than the way the dictionary defines the word. According to the authors, why is it so difficult to define "friend" precisely as it is used in American English?   [A]

2. What generalization do the authors make about the types of friends that many Americans have?   [B]

3. According to the authors, how do many Americans behave with others, even if they are strangers?   [C]
   a. They tend to be shy.
   b. They tend to smile.
   c. They tend to talk easily.
   d. Both (b) and (c).

4. What do the authors say about the way men and women socialize in the United States?   [F]

*The capital letters in brackets refer to the corresponding paragraphs in the reading.

5. In the United States, marriage relationships are: [G]

   a. all the same.

   b. different from couple to couple.

   c. arranged.

6. The authors say that in the United States remarriage is considered normal, and they point out that grown sons and daughters
often encourage their widowed or divorced parents to: [H]

   a. stay home alone.

   b. buy gold.

   c. continue to socialize.

7. The authors mention that in recent years the number of single
people in the United States has increased. What are two reasons
for this?   [I]

8. What are three of the ways that the authors say single people can
meet?   [K, L]

9. The authors say that one out of every five American families
moves every year because they: [M]

   a. get married.

   b. go to college in a different city.

   c. change jobs.

   d. all of the above.

10. What do the authors say can happen to relationships that are
only based on a common activity?   [N]

11. According to the authors, what is one of the most frequent problems in cross-cultural relationships?   [O]

12. According to the authors, Americans are sometimes shy with foreigners partly due to their:

   a. linguistic isolation.

   b. high considerateness.

   c. geographic location.

   d. both (a) and (c).

13. The authors say that the Americans' need for privacy is sometimes judged negatively by people who have not been raised with
the value of: [Q]

      a. group involvement.

      b. individualism.

      c. freedom.

14. According to the authors, how do many Americans feel when a friend becomes too dependent on them?   [R]

15. The authors say that when some Americans have problems, they like to have some time alone so that they can: [S]

      a. relax, read a book, and forget about their troubles.

      b. try to solve their problem by themselves.

      c. call several hospitals to find some answers.

16. The authors describe a situation in which people from different cultures had different expectations of their friendship. What did the American expect of his friend? What did the Russian expect of his friend?   [T, U]

17. According to the authors, what are the necessary ingredients for a true friendship?   [V]

18. What is one of the benefits that the authors say may come from socializing with people from the same culture?   [X]

19. What is one of the benefits that the authors say may come from socializing with people from different cultures?   [X]

Discussion Questions

Students should prepare these before class discussion.

1. In Paragraph A, the authors say that by using the word "friend," Americans do not specify the quality of the friendship that is mentioned. In other words, "friend" describes a variety of relationships. In your language, does this word have more than one meaning? Explain.

2. In Paragraph B, the authors say that "Americans have less time to pursue many close friends." According to the authors, what are the reasons for this?

3. In Paragraph C, the authors suggest that Americans have a certain reputation in some parts of the world. What is this reputation? Have you had experiences that support this?

4. Are people from your country open or private with information about themselves? How might they react to the American openness described in Paragraph E?

5. In Paragraph F, the authors describe various relationships between men and women in the United States. In your country, does an unmarried couple ever live together before they are married? Is it acceptable for people of the opposite sex to live together as roommates or housemates? Do you know Americans who are living together? Are they a couple, or do they live together for different reasons? Discuss.

6. In Paragraph G, the authors say that some married men and women consider themselves to be best friends. Do you think this is true of American couples that you have met? In your country, is this a common way to feel about one's spouse?

7. In Paragraph I, the authors discuss the increase in the number of single people in the United States. Does this mean that fewer people are choosing marriage? Why do you think people marry later or not at all?

8. According to the discussion in Paragraphs I and J, how do unmarried Americans feel when people ask them why they are not married? To what cultural value do the authors attribute the Americans' reaction?

9. In Paragraph L, the authors say that social networks offer opportunities to meet new people. Do Americans you know meet people through their friends? What are other ways that Americans meet people?

10. In the section about mobility and friendship in Paragraphs M and N, the authors note that people sometimes begin and end friendships quickly. Have you experienced this "quick" type of friendship with Americans? Did you know why it was "quick"?

11. Why do the authors say in Paragraph N that it is difficult for people from different cultures to understand why some American friendships are temporary?

12. In Paragraph P, the authors advise that in order to make an American friend, a foreigner should approach the American first. What specific advice would you give people from your country who wanted to make friends from your culture?

13. The authors tell a story about a friendship between a Russian and an American in Paragraphs T and U. Did the two men want to end the friendship? Why did it end? Have you ever had to adjust your expectations of a cross-cultural friendship in order to save it?

14. In Paragraph V, the authors talk about ways to understand the deeper culture of a country. What do they mean by "deeper" culture?

Vocabulary Exercises

Vocabulary List

As you read the vocabulary list below, find two or three words you already know. Give their definitions.

Paragraph A	*Paragraph B*	*Paragraph C*
acquaintance	casual	friendliness
precisely	commitment	friendship
	superficial	disclose
	pursue	encounters

Paragraph D	*Paragraph E*	*Paragraph F*
revealed	rarity	socialize
		limited
		practical
		compatible

Paragraph G	*Paragraph H*	*Paragraph I*
arranged	stigma	necessity

Paragraph J	*Paragraph K*	*Paragraph L*
innocent	mutual	social networks
	partners	exorbitant
	random	

Paragraph M	*Paragraph N*	*Paragraph O*
mobile	fade	extending
relocate	enduring	intended
	transient	

Paragraph P	*Paragraph Q*	*Paragraph R*
initiating	avoid	occurrence

Paragraph S	*Paragraph T*	*Paragraph U*
bothering	willingness	expectations
	financial	perspective
	repay	behaves

Paragraph V	*Paragraph X*
beneficial	assist
obvious	acculturation
	ultimately

Phrases and Expressions

strike up [C]: initiate; begin

golden years [H]: the years after middle age

sympathy calls [R]: telephone calls in which one person shows an interest and concern in another person's problems

work out [S]: solve a problem; find a solution to a conflict

A. Definitions

Choose the correct word for the definition from the list below. Then fill in the blanks in the sentences following the definitions. *Note: You may have to change the grammatical form of the word used in the sentence.*

acquaintance [A]	partners [K]
revealed [D]	exorbitant [L]
rarity [E]	occurrence [R]
compatible [F]	bothering [S]
necessity [I]	ultimately [X]
mutual [K]	

1. Definition: a person who takes part in an activity such as busi

   ness with another _____

   Unfortunately, the man's business _____ caused him to lose thousands of dollars.

2. Definition: a person someone knows _____

   Most people say, "Hi!" to friends and _____.

3. Definition: discovered; made clear _____

   At the end of the movie, the woman _____ her true identity.

4. Definition: shared; common _____

   They went to lunch with a _____ friend whom they both had known since they were ten years old.

5. Definition: something or someone that is uncommon, unusual, or

   special _____

   A winter with snow in Los Angeles is a _____ .

6. Definition: annoying; disturbing _____

If you do not stop _____ me, I will never finish this report.

7. Definition: able to cooperate and get along

   The two new friends were _____ , so they spent a lot of time together.

8. Definition: something that is required or essential

   Your passport is a _____ travel document.

9. Definition: finally; conclusively _____

   _____, the famous scientist ended her speech with an urgent message for world peace.

10. Definition: incident; happening _____

    Meeting my friend from childhood was a surprise _____.

11. Definition: extremely expensive; excessively high priced

    _____

    The _____ cost of train travel in America prevents many people from taking their families on train trips.

B. Word Forms

Choose the correct word form for each sentence. Change the original word to the appropriate form.

1. mobile   [M]

   a. Sociologists are studying the high rate of _____ in the United States.

   b. Some American families must be _____ because many jobs require movement to a new location every year.

2. superficial   [B]

   a. The teacher gave a _____ explanation that was not helpful.

   b. Some people show their interest _____.

   c. The young woman stopped dating her boyfriend because she did not like his _____ .

3. socialize   [F]

   a. The business partners also saw each other _____.

    b. If you want _____ , you must not be shy.

    c. What _____ activities are available to university students?

4. relocate [M]

    a. The cost of the company's _____ was very high.

    b. Mr. Smith liked his new job, but he became unhappy when his boss asked him _____ to a different office.

    c. Eventually, the family _____ near some relatives.

5. initiating [P]

    a. It is not easy _____ a friendship.

    b. The _____ step in breaking a habit is knowing that you want to break it.

    c. The school is _____ a new attendance system.

6. precisely [A]

    a. The amount of flour must be _____ if you want to make bread successfully.

    b. Using a word _____ can be difficult, even if you know the meaning.

    c. It is said that the _____ of a Swiss watch is perfect.

7. intended [O]

    a. The _____ of the student was to get good grades.

    b. I _____ to start a program of regular exercise tomorrow.

    c. We _____ to go to the dance last night, but we were too tired.

8. commitment [B]

    a. The business partners were clearly _____ to the project.

    b. She has a _____ to her grandmother, so she takes good care of her.

    c. If you cannot _____ to this date, let's make an appointment for another day.

9. arranged   [G]

    a. Maria's father came and helped her _____ the new furniture.

    b. The marriage was _____ many months ago.

    c. I have made _____ to have you driven to the train station at noon.

10. extending   [O]

    a. In America, the _____ family used to live and work near each other.

    b. According to the chapter, it is difficult for some foreigners to know when an American is _____ an offer for friendship.

    c. She asked her boss for an _____ on the report because she had not finished it.

11. avoid   [Q]

    a. Try to pay your bills if you want _____ problems with the bank.

    b. The police station made the young boy nervous, so he _____ going near it.

12. behaves   [U]

    a. Rude _____ will cause the loss of friends.

    b. The young child finally admitted that he had _____ poorly at school that day.

    c. A person who _____ politely will be admired.

13. beneficial   [V]

    a. Daily exercise can be _____ to your health.

    b. The _____ of good study habits are not immediate.

    c. Friday night, the symphony will give a _____ performance in order to raise money for the hospital.

C. Words in Sentences

Read the definition of the following words and note their part of speech. Then use each one in a sentence.

1. casual [B]: informal; relaxed

2. encounters [C]: meetings (usually by chance)

_____

3. limited [F]: restricted; confined

_____

4. innocent [J]: harmless; not guilty

_____

5. enduring [N]: lasting; long-term

_____

6. perspective [U]: point of view; opinion

_____

7. assist [X]: help; aid

_____

8. permanent [V]: lasting; unchangeable

_____

D. Matching

Match the words with their definitions. Place the letter of the definition in the space next to the word.

_____ pursue	a.	chance; without method
_____ disclose	b.	short-term; temporary
_____ friendship	c.	adaptation
_____ practical	d.	easily understandable; clear
	e.	useful; efficient
_____ stigma	f.	to go after; to attempt to make
_____ random	g.	negative label
_____ fade	h.	expose
_____ transient	i.	a relationship in which people know, like, and trust each other
_____ obvious	j.	disappear gradually
_____ adjustment	k.	behavior characterized by smiling, chattiness, and warmth
_____ friendliness		

E. Fill-In

First review the way the following words are used in Paragraphs T and U. Then fill in each of the blanks in the paragraph below with the word that best fits the sentence. *Note: Change the part of speech when necessary.*

willingness   [T]
financial   [T]
repay   [T]
expectations   [U]

The story of the Russian immigrant and his American friend shows how different _____ can create misunderstandings. The American was _____ to help his friend, but he did not want to sign a paper that said he would _____ a loan. The American felt that the _____ obligations of his Russian friend were not his concern, so he preferred to remain uninvolved in his friend's finances.

F. Phrases and Expressions

1. Someone who wants to strike up a conversation wants to: [C]
   a. start a conversation.
   b. have an argument.
   c. discuss baseball.
   d. end a conversation.

2. When American people refer to their *golden years*, they are talking about the time when they will: [H]
   a. have good luck.
   b. be older.
   c. be wealthier.

3. Someone who telephones to give you a "sympathy call" wants to: [R]
   a. Apologize for something he or she has done.
   b. Say that you are nice.
   c. Show they understand your situation.

Conversational Activities

A. Proverbs and Quotations

A "proverb" is a short, popular saying expressing a well-known truth. A "quotation" is a passage that is taken word for word from the author. Proverbs and quotations serve to communicate attitudes, values, and beliefs. The following is a list of proverbs and quotations on the theme of friendship. Read them and discuss the questions that follow.

Quotations

Friendship is the inexpressible comfort of feeling safe with a person having neither to weigh thoughts nor measure words.

George Eliot, pen name for Mary Ann Evans
(English novelist, 1819–1880)

Don't walk in front of me
    I may not follow
Don't walk behind me
    I may not lead
Walk beside me
            And just be my friend.

Albert Camus (French writer
born in Algeria, 1913–1960)

Proverbs

German

    In trade and commerce, friendship ceases.

    When you require nothing, go to your friends.

Arabic

    If your friend be honey, do not eat him.

    Don't wash the cup of friendship with vinegar.

Spanish

    There is no better mirror than an old friend.

    Among soldiers and friends, compliments are superfluous.

Persian

> It is rest to take trouble for a friend.
>
> One is never a friend by force.

English

> You may find your worst enemy or best friend in yourself.
>
> Make new friends and keep the old; one is silver and the other gold.

Discuss

> What do these quotations and proverbs suggest about the meaning of friendship?
>
> Do you know any other proverbs on friendship?

B. Questions About Friendship

Friendship is universal; a close friend is a close friend anywhere. There are qualities we all admire in friends, and things all of us would do for friends. The purpose of the following questions is to enable you to share your views on friendship with other class members. Answer the questions individually, and then discuss your responses in small groups. Which questions elicit a wide variety of responses? Do you think any of the responses are influenced by culture?

1. In your country, where, when, or how did you first meet most of your friends? Circle as many as apply.

   a. childhood   f. jobs

   b. within the family   g. neighbors

   c. sports   h. college or university

   d. organizations   i. other friends

   e. schools   j. other

2. How many years have you known your closest friend?

   a. less than one year

   b. one to five years

   c. five to twelve years

   d. twelve to twenty years

   e. more than twenty years

3. In your country, did you have close friends from different countries? If so, which countries?

4. Are your friends members of other religious groups? If so, which religions?

5. Are most of your close friends the same sex as you or the opposite sex?

   a. my sex

   b. half are men, and half are women

   c. opposite sex

6. In your country are there any societal attitudes that encourage or discourage friendships between people of the opposite sex?

7. Are friendships between people of the opposite sex different from friendships between people of the same sex? If so, how?

8. Are most of your friends:

   a. married men

   b. married women

   c. single men

   d. single women

   e. married couples

9. Do you prefer going out with a group of friends or with one or two friends? Explain your preferences.

10. In your country, do couples (married or unmarried) usually go out with groups of people, with one other couple, or alone?

11. Circle the five qualities that you think are the most important in a friend.

    a. sense of humor

    b. intelligence

    c. warmth

    d. physical beauty

    e. loyalty

    f. independence (i.e., not being too dependent on you)

    g. complete honesty

    h. similar religious beliefs

    i. similar political beliefs

    j. similar educational background

12. Which of the following actions would probably end a friendship of yours? Circle all that apply.

    a. your lending money to a friend and not getting it back

    b. a friend becoming involved with someone the other didn't like

     c. you or the other person getting married

     d. you or the other person having children

     e. you or the other person getting divorced

     f. you or the other person changing political views

     g. you or the other person changing religious views

     h. you or the other person moving away

     i. one friend becoming more successful than the other

13. Have you ever lost a friend for any of the above reasons? Are there other reasons for which friends terminate their relationships?

C. Case Studies

Divide into small groups of three to five people and analyze the following case studies.* First have someone *read* the case study aloud. Second, try to *identify* the problem(s) and the misinterpretation(s) described. Use the follow-up questions to aid your discussion. Finally, choose someone to *summarize* your discussion for the rest of the class.

A Date with Mona[2]

John: An American student abroad

Mona: A classmate from the country in which John is studying

John, an American, is abroad studying history and languages. It is in his history class that he becomes friendly with a young woman, Mona. John soon discovers that Mona's father is one of the country's well-known historians and that he has written several books. Since John is interested in history, Mona invites him to her home to have dinner and meet her family. The warmth and friendliness of the family are exceeded only by the huge feast Mona's mother prepares. John is very happy. He doesn't have much chance to meet Mona's mother and sisters since they eat in another room. Nevertheless, he has a pleasant discussion with her father and two brothers. Later that evening, he is able to talk with Mona in her parents' presence.

    A few weeks later Mona invites John to another elaborate meal and discussion with her father. Again, the women disappear after

*Case studies are usually brief stories about everyday occurrences that contain a problem for groups to solve. Intercultural case studies are primarily used to gain insight into cultural problems and to discover ways of resolving conflicts of values, attitudes, or feelings.

serving the meal. However, this time the father and brothers must leave early. Mona joins John, and they spend the evening talking alone in the living room while Mona's mother is working in the kitchen.

John wants to express his appreciation to Mona and invites her to his apartment for dinner. John tells Mona that although he lives alone in a small apartment and cooking is difficult, he would like to try cooking a meal for her. He jokingly tells Mona, "Maybe you can teach me how to prepare your food properly!" Suddenly, Mona gets very angry and says, "I didn't know you thought I was that kind of girl!" She walks away, almost crying. John asks himself, "What did I do wrong?"

Discuss

1. Why is Mona hurt and angry?
2. What special rules or customs seem to govern hospitality and eating in Mona's family?
3. John thought that he could extend this kind of dinner invitation to an American woman, and so he assumed he could do the same with Mona. What was wrong with his assumption?
4. What do you think are the rules governing male-female relationships in Mona's culture? What other ways might John have shown his appreciation to Mona?

A Friend of a Friend[3]

Michael: An American graduate student abroad

Mr. Umm: Michael's best friend in the foreign country

Mr. Tahh: Mr. Umm's older friend

Michael is a graduate student in a foreign university. He is a good friend of Mr. Umm, who lives in the dormitory for graduate students. They share a similar sense of humor and enjoy many activities together. Since Michael is interested in architecture, Mr. Umm decides that it would be a good idea for Michael to meet his older friend Mr. Tahh, a professor of design at the university. First, he tells Michael all about Mr. Tahh's architectural research. As it turns out, Mr. Tahh's research is exactly what Michael needs for his thesis.

Michael is so excited that the next day he goes directly to Mr. Tahh's office, introduces himself, and briefly mentions Mr. Umm's name. The two men spend several hours discussing their research ideas.

That evening Michael tells Mr. Umm how much he enjoyed meeting Mr. Tahh. Mr. Umm reacts coldly, "Yes, I heard you both met. I hope your research goes well." His serious tone tells Michael that something is wrong, but Michael has no idea what the problem might be.

Discuss

1. First analyze Mr. Umm's reaction and Michael's confusion. Then consider the following questions:
2. What do you think might be the rules for introductions to Mr. Umm's culture?
3. Michael met Mr. Tahh as he might have met a professor in his American university. Why was this inappropriate in Mr. Umm's culture? How might Michael have avoided the problem?

At an American Party

Malita and Palil: A newly arrived immigrant couple in the United States

Jan: Malita and Palil's sponsor in the United States

Malita and Palil, newly arrived immigrants in the United States, are eager to make friends. Jan, their sponsor, has promised them that she will have a party and invite several of her friends so that they can meet people. When she does have the party, a number of people talk to Malita and Palil, and show an interest in them and their culture. At the end of the party, many people say, "It was nice meeting you; I hope to see you again." This made the new couple feel very good. There were even three people who asked them for their phone number. Malita and Palil felt that it would be very easy to make friends in the United States.

Several weeks passed after the party, but nobody had called them except Jan. They wanted to ask their friend why the other Americans were so friendly but didn't call. However, the new couple felt too hurt and had too much pride to ask.

Discuss

1. Analyze the problem the newcomers faced.
2. Why did the Americans' behavior give the couple the feeling that it would be easy to make friends in the United States? (Recall the concepts of friendliness and friendship from the reading.)
3. How can you explain the fact that the Americans didn't call the couple after the party?

4. Is there anything that Malita or Palil could have done to show that they were interested in having further contact with the people they met at the party? In other words, how could they have made the first move or taken the initiative?

D. Multiple-Choice Questionnaire

The following questions are intended to stimulate cross-cultural discussion and to help you become familiar with American customs and responses. First, write an answer that describes a likely response in your country. On the multiple-choice questions, try to guess what an American would do. *More than one answer may be correct.*

1. If you were invited to another family's house for dinner, how much later than the scheduled time would you arrive?

In your country: _____

In the United States:

a. Fifteen minutes later

b. Thirty minutes later

c. One hour later

d. Two or more hours later

2. How long does a party at which dinner is served usually last?

In your country: _____

In the United States:

a. One to two hours

b. Three to four hours

c. Five to six hours

d. Seven to eight hours

3. If you were having a party for the students in your class, how many days in advance would you invite them?

In your country: _____

In the United States:

a. The day of the party

b. One day in advance

c. Several days in advance

d. 3 or 4 weeks in advance

4. How would a host indicate to a guest that it was time to leave?

In your country: _____

In the United States:

a. The host would start yawning.

b. The host would announce, "It's time to leave."

c. The host would start cleaning up.

d. The host wouldn't say anything, so I would leave at a time I thought was reasonable.

5. At a party or other social occasion, how would you indicate that it was time for you to leave someone's home?

In your country: _____

In the United States:

a. I would wait until the host said something.

b. I would say, "I'm sorry. I have to leave now."

c. I would say, "It's getting late, and I'd better be going."

d. I would make up an excuse (e.g., I have to get up early tomorrow) and thank the host.

E. The Singles Scene: An American Dating Agency

A profile from "Great Expectations," a very popular dating service in almost forty cities in the United States appears on p. 165.[4] Read the form and answer the following questions:

1. Does this type of organization that matches singles exist in your culture?

2. If it does, is it as widely used as it is in the United States?

3. Do you think this is a good way for people to meet each other? Why or why not?

F. Cross-Cultural Questions

1. If dating is an institution in your country, when do people begin to date? Are the rules for dating the same for men and women?

2. What are common dating activities? Are chaperones present on dates? What role do parents play in dating? Does the man have to meet the parents before he takes the woman out?

3. If dating is not common in your country, how are marriage partners found or arranged?

4. Discuss other living arrangements that are common in your culture. Besides married men and women, who else lives together (for example, unmarried couples, nonromantic friends of the opposite sex, homosexuals, etc.)? How common are these alternative living arrangements and relationships? Are they sanctioned by your culture?

Cultural Notes

1. In the United States the terms "boyfriend" and "girlfriend" are used differently depending on which sex uses the words. If a man uses the term "girlfriend" or a woman uses the term "boyfriend," romantic involvement is implied. However, a woman may say, "I'm going to meet my girlfriend today"

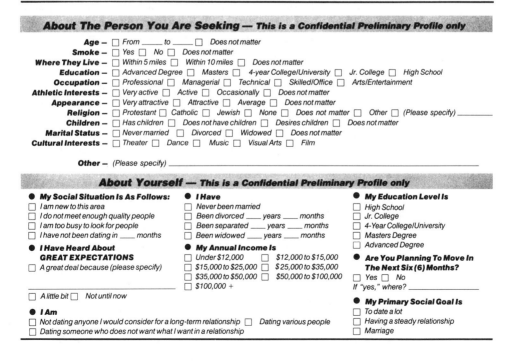

GREAT ≋ EXPECTATIONS SINGLES PROFILE FORM™

About The Person You Are Seeking — This is a Confidential Preliminary Profile only

Age – ☐ From _____ to _____ ☐ *Does not matter*
Smoke – ☐ *Yes* ☐ *No* ☐ *Does not matter*
Where They Live – ☐ *Within 5 miles* ☐ *Within 10 miles* ☐ *Does not matter*
Education – ☐ *Advanced Degree* ☐ *Masters* ☐ *4-year College/University* ☐ *Jr. College* ☐ *High School*
Occupation – ☐ *Professional* ☐ *Managerial* ☐ *Technical* ☐ *Skilled/Office* ☐ *Arts/Entertainment*
Athletic Interests – ☐ *Very active* ☐ *Active* ☐ *Occasionally* ☐ *Does not matter*
Appearance – ☐ *Very attractive* ☐ *Attractive* ☐ *Average* ☐ *Does not matter*
Religion – ☐ *Protestant* ☐ *Catholic* ☐ *Jewish* ☐ *None* ☐ *Does not matter* ☐ *Other* ☐ *(Please specify)* _____
Children – ☐ *Has children* ☐ *Does not have children* ☐ *Desires children* ☐ *Does not matter*
Marital Status – ☐ *Never married* ☐ *Divorced* ☐ *Widowed* ☐ *Does not matter*
Cultural Interests – ☐ *Theater* ☐ *Dance* ☐ *Music* ☐ *Visual Arts* ☐ *Film*

Other – *(Please specify)* _____

About Yourself — This is a Confidential Preliminary Profile only

● **My Social Situation Is As Follows:**
☐ *I am new to this area*
☐ *I do not meet enough quality people*
☐ *I am too busy to look for people*
☐ *I have not been dating in ____ months*

● **I Have Heard About GREAT EXPECTATIONS**
☐ *A great deal because (please specify)*
_____
☐ *A little bit* ☐ *Not until now*

● **I Am**
☐ *Not dating anyone I would consider for a long-term relationship* ☐ *Dating various people*
☐ *Dating someone who does not want what I want in a relationship*

● **I Have**
☐ *Never been married*
☐ *Been divorced ____ years ____ months*
☐ *Been separated ____ years ____ months*
☐ *Been widowed ____ years ____ months*

● **My Annual Income Is**
☐ *Under $12,000* ☐ *$12,000 to $15,000*
☐ *$15,000 to $25,000* ☐ *$25,000 to $35,000*
☐ *$35,000 to $50,000* ☐ *$50,000 to $100,000*
☐ *$100,000 +*

● **My Education Level Is**
☐ *High School*
☐ *Jr. College*
☐ *4-Year College/University*
☐ *Masters Degree*
☐ *Advanced Degree*

● **Are You Planning To Move In The Next Six (6) Months?**
☐ *Yes* ☐ *No*
If "yes," where? _____

● **My Primary Social Goal Is**
☐ *To date a lot*
☐ *Having a steady relationship*
☐ *Marriage*

(meaning a close friend), but most males would *not* say, "I'm going to meet my boyfriend." Instead, they would say, "I'm going to meet a friend of mine today."

2. Traditionally, the man took the initiative to invite a woman on a date. This tradition is changing, and it is becoming more common for a woman to ask a man out. The invitation does not always imply a romantic interest, but may be a way of getting to know someone.

3. A changing custom that can create problems for both men and women is the question of who pays for whom on dates. Traditionally men have paid the expenses on dates, regardless of whether the couple's relationship is intimate or merely friendly. Currently, some women feel more comfortable paying for themselves and may occasionally pay for the man. "Dutch treat" refers to a date where each individual pays for himself or herself. There are no fixed rules for payment.

4. There is a large homosexual, or "gay," population in the United States, and, especially in certain cities (e.g., San Francisco), members of the gay community are open about their sexual identity. Newcomers in the United States often have a difficult time accepting and understanding this openness because, in most societies, homosexuality is taboo, even though it exists all over the world. It is beyond the scope of this book to discuss this aspect of personal relationships, but it is worthwhile explaining that for many, being American means having the freedom to express themselves individually and to choose the life style that they want. Many Americans pride themselves in the fact that they do not have to conform and that their society is open enough to allow for diversity. While many Americans do not approve of homosexuality, some have learned to accept the diversity and to see beyond a person's sexual preferences. In other words, a person's homosexuality does not make him or her any less of a contributing, productive member of society. There are gays in almost every profession, socioeconomic level, and ethnic group in the United States. Those who are new to the United States must realize that it is offensive to make fun of members of this community, just as it is insensitive to make racial or ethnic jokes. The American ideal teaches respect and equality for all individuals, no matter what the background or life style.

Supplementary Vocabulary and Phrases

to confide in someone	to be engaged to someone
to trust someone	to let someone down

to rely on someone
to feel comfortable with someone
to empathize with someone
to sympathize with someone
to be hurt by someone
to be disappointed in someone

to reciprocate
common interests
loneliness
fiancé, fiancée
affection

Household Composition: 1970 to 1988[1]

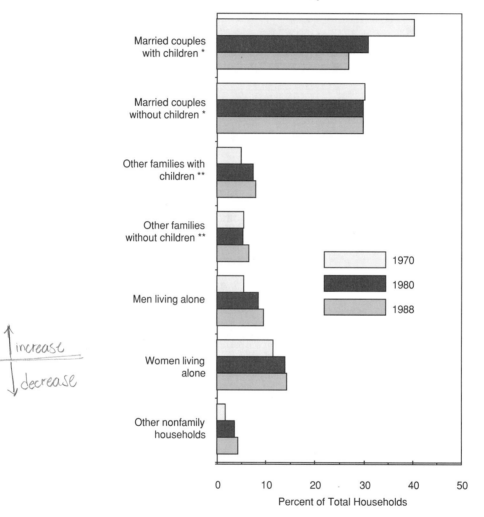

increase
decrease

*Own children under 18.
**"Other families" include single parents, relatives, friends, and any combination of people who are not married to each other.

6

Family: Types and Traditions

"How many different things a family can be—a nest of tenderness, a jail for the heart, a nursery of souls. Families name us and define us, give us strength, give us grief. All our lives we struggle to embrace or escape their influence. They are magnets that both hold us close and drive us away. And yet, is there anything we take for granted more than family?"[2]

Pre-Reading Discussion

1. In your opinion, does the quote above define all families? Is there anything about it that is not universal? Would it be an accurate characterization of families in your culture?

2. Look at the graph showing household composition in the United States from 1970 to 1988. First discuss the categories and the changes over the years. Then compare the information with your knowledge of household composition in your culture.

3. For you, what defines a family? Who is in your family? What are your obligations to family members?

4. Did your parents have a great deal of authority over you when you were younger? How old were you when you were allowed to make your own decisions? What types of decisions could you make? Do you think American children generally have more or less freedom than children in your culture?

5. In your country, whose responsibility is it to take care of an elderly person who becomes very sick? What expectations does society have about care for the elderly?

Pre-Reading Vocabulary

1. Definitions
   a. **nuclear family**: the mother, father, sisters, and brothers
   b. **extended family**: the family members "outside" of the nuclear family, including grandparents, aunts, uncles, cousins, nephews, nieces, and in-laws (relatives through marriage)

   Discussion: In the United States, nuclear families generally live in homes without members of the extended family. Who lives in the typical family home in your country? What members of your family are most involved in your life?

2. Definition

   autonomy: independence; control over one's life

   Discussion: Are children in your country taught to seek autonomy from their families? At what age do they usually leave their parents' home? How does this compare to the American practice, according to your knowledge?

3. Definition

   the elderly: the population of the very old

   Discussion: Are the elderly in your country kept separate from or integrated into society? What observations have you made about the elderly in America?

4. Definition

   single-parent family: a family consisting of the children and one parent, either the father or the mother (in the United States, it is usually the mother)

   Discussion: Due to the high divorce rate in the United States, there are many single-parent families. Do you know any single-parent American families? Are there many such families in your culture?

Skimming: For General Information

To get the general idea of the reading that follows:

1. Read the titles and headings of the sections.

2. Read the first and last paragraphs of the reading.

From your skimming, answer the following:

1. Do families in all cultures meet the needs of their members in the same way?

2. Is there only one type of American family?

Scanning: For Specific Information

To find specific information in the reading, look for clues such as certain words and numbers. Scan the reading to find the answers to the following:

1. At what age do American children leave their family to begin an independent life?

2. What percentage of women between the ages of sixty-eight and seventy-four years live alone?

3. What is the divorce rate in the United States?

Reading Text

Family: Types and Traditions

[A]   There are universal °dimensions of family life, and the functions of a
family are similar around the world. However, families' structures
and their methods of satisfying human needs differ greatly. For example, one needs only to observe how parents talk to their young, how
5   children respond to their parents, and the degree to which children's
independence is encouraged or discouraged to know that there are
significant cross-cultural differences among families.

Child Raising

[B]   Acculturation, which begins at birth, is the process of teaching new
generations of children the customs and values of the parents' culture. How people treat newborns, for example, is °indicative of cultural values. In the United States, it is common for parents to put a
5   newborn in a separate bedroom when the child is a few weeks old.
Part of the reason is economic; that is, many houses are large enough
to offer each child a separate room. However, Americans have other

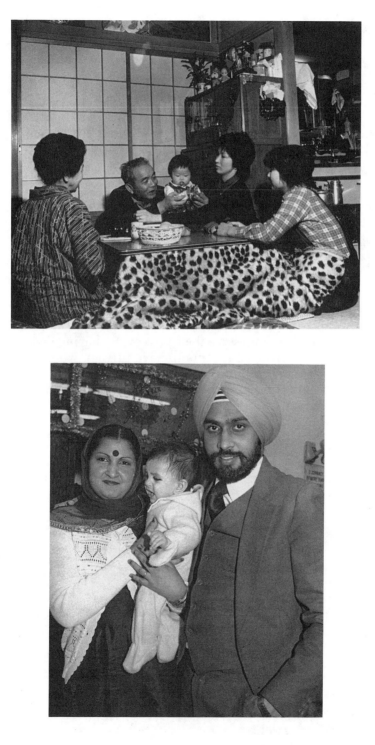

reasons for separating their children physically soon after birth. Parents like to preserve their privacy. By having their own rooms, the children will also be able to have privacy when they are older. In addition, the children will eventually learn to be responsible for their own living space. This is seen as a first step toward personal independence.

[C]   Americans have traditionally held independence and the closely related value of individualism in high °esteem. Parents try to °instill

these values in their children. American English expresses these value preferences: at a certain age, children should °"cut the (umbilical) cord" and are encouraged not to be °"tied to their mothers' apron strings." In the process of their socialization, children learn to °"look out for number one" and to °"stand on their own two feet."

[D]   Many children are taught at an early age to make decisions and to be responsible for their actions. Often children work for money outside the home as a first step to establishing °autonomy. Some ten-year-olds, for example, mow their neighbors' lawns, and slightly older children may deliver newspapers or babysit. This type of work is encouraged by parents, who see it as a means for their children to learn the "value of a dollar" as well as learn responsibility.

Young Adulthood

[E]   Upon reaching a certain age (usually between eighteen and twenty-one years), American children have typically been encouraged, but usually not forced, to °"leave the nest" and begin independent lives. However, contrary to the stereotype held by many foreigners, over 50 percent of young adults aged eighteen to twenty-four currently live in their parents' home.[3] Young people seem to be "leaving the nest" later, largely for economic reasons. After children leave home they

often find social relationships and financial support outside the family. (There is, however, a great deal of variation among ethnic groups;
10 members of some groups continue to support their children financially for many years into adulthood.) Parents do not arrange marriages for their children, nor do children usually ask their parents' permission to get married. Romantic love is most often the basis for marriage in the United States; young adults meet their future °spouses through
15 other friends, at school, at work, and in organizations and religious institutions. Although children choose their own spouses, they still hope that their parents will approve of their choices.

[F]   In many families, parents feel that children should make major life decisions by themselves. A parent may try to influence a child to follow a particular profession, but the child is free to choose another °career. Sometimes children do precisely the opposite of what their
5 parents wish in order to assert their independence. A son, for example, may °deliberately decide not to go into his father's business because of a fear that he will lose his autonomy. Independence from parents is seen as positive; parents and children love each other even with the independence that characterizes their relationship. Many
10 parents feel that they have done a good job raising their children if their children are °self-reliant by the time they reach twenty-one.

The Elderly

[G] Societal and familial °treatment of the °elderly also reflects the values of independence and individualism. Their financial support is often provided by government-sponsored °social security or welfare systems that decrease their dependence on the family. Additionally,
5 older people often seek their own friends rather than becoming too emotionally dependent on their children. °Senior citizen centers provide a means for °peer-group association within their age group. There are problems, however, with growing old in the United States. °Indifference to the aged and °glorification of youth have left some
10 old people °alienated and alone. It is estimated that 15 percent of men aged sixty-five to seventy-four and 35 percent of women in the same age group live alone.[4]

[H]   It is a common practice for families to place their older relatives in nursing homes because of physical disabilities or illness rather than caring for them in their homes. This is, however, less common for those cultural groups within the United States whose values
5 include fulfilling obligations to the extended family. Yet, some "nonethnic" families (i.e., those who typically emphasize obligations to the °nuclear family rather than to the °extended family) are realizing that the care in many nursing homes is inadequate, and thus they

are looking for better alternatives to nursing homes. Some middle-age
10   children provide care for older relatives in their own homes, while
others attempt to find nursing care for them in their parents' own
homes. The ideal situation is when parents can stay in their own
homes even if they cannot care for themselves. Many older people do
not want to have to rely on their grown children. The same spirit of
15   independence that guides °child raising and young adulthood affects
older people. If given a choice (financial status is a large considera-
tion), many older people would choose to live in °retirement communities where they have the companionship of peers and many recre-
ational and health services. The disadvantage of this type of living
20   arrangement is that it results in a separation of the generations. Some
people see this as psychologically unhealthy; others prefer the separation.

The Nuclear and the Extended Family

[I]   Attitudes toward the elderly can be further understood by °distin-
guishing between "nuclear" and "extended" family structures. In the

United States, the nuclear family consists of the father, the mother, and the children; this is "the family." The extended family, which

5 consists of grandparents, aunts, uncles, cousins, nephews, nieces, and in-laws, is important in the United States, but in different ways than in other cultures. Members of the extended family are not necessarily consulted when it comes to making major decisions, and it is not assumed that extended family members will take care of the children

10 in the family. (Although in single-parent families, there is sometimes more reliance on extended family members.) In some other cultures, it is assumed that extended family members will take care of older members, have intensive contact with relatives, and establish °communal living.

[J]   The distinction between the nuclear and the extended family is important because it suggests the extent of family °ties and °obligations. In extended families, the children and parents have strong obligations to other relatives. In the United States, there are close ties to

5 some extended family members (especially to grandparents), but not the same obligations that you would find in other cultures. Again,

this varies among members of ethnic groups. For example, Italian-Americans, Chinese-Americans, Jewish-Americans, and Mexican-Americans, among others, have more extensive obligations and con-
10 tact with extended family members than do many other Americans.
[K] The American nuclear family usually has its own separate °residence and is often economically independent of other family members. When couples marry, they are expected to live independently of their parents and become "heads of households" when they have
5 children. In times of financial need, it is not unusual for nuclear family members to °borrow money from a bank rather than from relatives. Unlike practices in some other cultures, many couples struggle to buy their own first home without expecting family members to contribute. When older parents help their married children with the
10 "down payment" (the initial payment for a house), it is appreciated but not expected. Among members of some ethnic groups in the United States (e.g., Chinese-Americans and Filipino-Americans), extended family members often °"pool" their money so that a young couple can buy a home.

Working Wives and Husbands

[L] In both nuclear and extended families, the culture °imposes set gender roles upon parents. Traditionally, the male was responsible for the financial support of the home and family members, and the female was responsible for emotional support, child raising, and
5 housekeeping. However, during the past two to three decades in the United States, gender roles have been redefined, with an increasing number of mothers in the work force. The °prescribed roles of the man as the °"breadwinner" and the woman as the housewife have changed dramatically. A major reason for this change is the women's
10 movement, which has influenced society's views of desirable educational goals and careers for women. In addition, because of financial necessity, it is often no longer possible for a family to live on one salary.
[M] It is estimated that both spouses work in 63 percent of American marriages where there are children aged six to seventeen. (The figure is about 51 percent for parents with children under six.)[5] For many women, their work represents the need to contribute to the family
5 income and not a means of attaining personal fulfillment. These women are often carrying an extra burden. They work outside the home, yet they are still primarily responsible for the maintenance and care of the household and children. Other women choose to work because they want to share in providing financial support for the
10 family. In addition, they want to pursue their °professional interests

in order to fulfill themselves and to contribute to the larger society (i.e., not just to their family.)

[N]   A <u>challenge</u> for couples with children is finding °day care and obtaining flexible work schedules so that they can coordinate their time between home and work. Occasionally, husbands stay home and care for the children and home while the wives work. For most cou-
5 ples, changing work patterns involves °negotiating home and family tasks. Some men, even those with wives who contribute to the family income, resist doing household and family tasks that have traditionally been characterized as "women's work." Among many younger people, however, this is changing.

*it's difficult
work hard to be
successful at*

[O]   In some cases, particularly among the highly educated, there are °"dual career couples" where both the husband and the wife work full-time in high-level professional jobs (e.g., lawyers, doctors, professors, and managers). In these families, there is generally a more °equi-
5 table sharing of family and home responsibilities than in the larger population.

[P]   Although they are not common, there are situations where both members of a couple cannot find employment in the same geographical location, and so one will move and °commute back to the family on weekends. In a minority of cases, people have to fly great dis-
5 tances to maintain such °"commuter marriages." This can be a strain

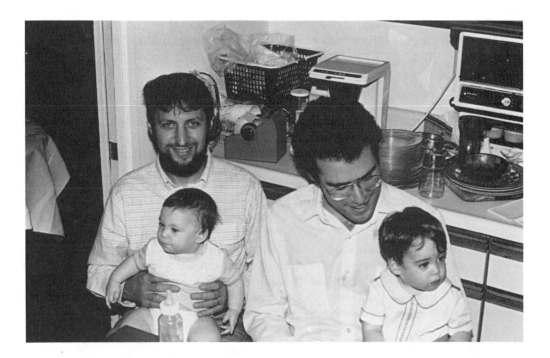

on the family, but both the husband and the wife are strongly committed to their respective professions. Some couples believe that their
family life is better because they make the most of the little "family
time" that they have.

Single-Parent Families

[Q] Changes in the American family structure are evidenced by high rates
of separation and divorce. It is estimated that almost 50 percent of all
marriages end in divorce.[6] These trends have resulted in a high number of single-parent families headed mostly by women. Many of these
5   women do not receive °alimony or child support payments, and are
more likely to be poor than married women. Single mothers (and
fathers) often feel °"stretched to their limits" with the unending
responsibilities that face them. They carry the burden of supporting a
family and being totally responsible for their children. They have
10   very few opportunities for rest and relaxation, unless they have sup-
portive extended family members who will help them.

[R]   Despite the high numbers of single parents in the United States,
there is no indication that marriage is becoming less popular. The
remarriage rate remains high, with °approximately four out of five

divorced couples eventually remarrying other people.[7] When single
5   parents marry each other, they create "stepfamilies" or "blended families."

Varieties of Families in the United States

[S]   In the United States, there are now families that would not have been
called "families" fifty or one hundred years ago. The largest percentage is still the traditional family with two parents and children, but
this type is not even the majority of families in certain areas.
5   Children can belong to two families, for example, if their parents are
divorced. They may live with one parent for half the week and the
other parent during the second half of the week. A family may be a
°"blended" one in which both parents have been divorced, each with
their own children. They remarry and bring both sets of children into
10   the marriage. Two women or two men with or without children can
also °constitute a family. Couples who have decided not to have children or unmarried couples who have chosen to live together may

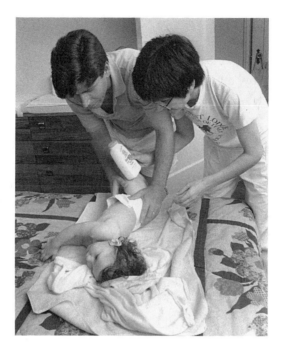

likewise see themselves as a "family." A single parent (e.g., divorced or widowed) having complete responsibility for the care of the chil-
15 dren would not want to be considered to have "less" of a family than someone in a family with two parents.

[T] The °regional, ethnic, and religious heterogeneity in the United States means that people will react differently to families that are nontraditional. Individuals also vary in their reactions to diversity in family type. (In other words, people within a region or an ethnic
5 group will disagree on what constitutes a family.) In general, on the West and East coasts, there is more tolerance for diversity in family structures than there is in the South or the Midwest. Also, in areas where people tend to be more religious, there seems to be less acceptance of the nontraditional family.

[U] The various family types found in the United States may not have much in common, but they do demonstrate that the family as an °institution is not dying. It is instead one that is changing and is being °accommodated by a society that does not enforce "sameness"
5 in family life style. The changes in the traditional family structure are seen by some as a breakdown or disintegration of values and a decline in °morality. Others, however, believe that these °shifts in family shape are inevitable in a rapidly changing society.

*Comprehension Questions**

1. The graph is used at the beginning of the chapter to show:
   a. how a house is built.
   (b) who lives in a house.
   c. family structure in the 1970s and 1980s.

2. In your opinion, does the graph reveal a significant sociological trend(s)? If so, what is the trend or trends?

3. According to the authors, acculturation is the process by which children learn the values and customs of the parents' culture. Parents put a newborn in a separate room when the child is a few weeks old because: [B]
   a. they want to have privacy.
   b. they don't like the noise.
   c. separation is seen as the first step toward personal independence.
   (d) both (a) and (c).

4. Financial independence is one way for American youths: [D]
   (a) to establish autonomy. = independence
   b. to rebel against their parents.
   c. to learn to deliver newspapers.

5. At what age are American children encouraged to begin an independent life? [E] between 18 & 21 years old.

6. Do American parents arrange the marriages of their children? [E] No. They let them choose their couple.

7. According to the authors, many American parents feel that their children should make major life decisions: [F]
   a. with the help of the entire family.
   (b) by themselves.
   c. with a computer.

8. The fact that many elderly people choose to live alone and away from their children reinforces the idea that: [G, H]
   a. American society is completely unconcerned with the elderly.
   b. the elderly are wealthy enough to live alone.

*The capital letters in brackets refer to the corresponding paragraphs in the reading.

(c.) the elderly often do not want to be dependent on their grown children.

9. Many older people would prefer to live in retirement communities because there they would have: [H]

    a. the companionship of their peers.

    b. recreational and health services.

    c. free bus rides.

    (d.) both (a) and (b).

10. The authors' distinction between nuclear and extended families: [J]

    a. enables the reader to understand the importance of grandparents.

    b. shows which kind of family is better.

    (c.) suggests the extent of family ties and obligations.

11. Are family obligations and ties the same for all ethnic groups in the United States? What examples do the authors give?
    No, depends of the cultures   pp. 178 & 179

12. When American couples marry, do they usually live with their parents or on their own?   [K]
    They live independently of their parents.

13. The roles of the man as the "breadwinner" and the woman as the housewife are: [L]

    a. permanent roles in the American family.

    b. traditional roles that do not apply to the American family.

    (c.) undergoing change in the American family.

14. What two main reasons do the authors give for the changing roles of husbands and wives?   [L]
    Women's movement, financial necessity

15. Is it easy for couples with children to coordinate their time between home and work?   [N] No.

16. What has been the result of the high rates of separation and divorce?   [Q]

    a. single-parent families headed mostly by men

    b. separated families

    (c.) single-parent families headed mostly by women

17. It is difficult to describe the "typical" American family because of: [S, T]

adjective.. heterogeneous
homogeneous – homogeneity

a. the regional, religious, and ethnic heterogeneity of people in the United States.

b. the religious influences on individual families.

c. economic conditions and job mobility.

18. The authors say that the changes in the traditional family structure: [U]

a. can be interpreted as a breakdown or as a result of a quickly changing society.

b. are the result of a "sick" society.

c. mean that the family is dying.

Discussion Questions

Students should prepare these before class discussion.

1. According to Paragraph D, why do American parents encourage their children to work at an early age? How old were you when you had your first job? Do you know Americans who have young children who work? What are their jobs?

2. In Paragraph E, the authors say that young adults are not usually forced to start an independent life. However, a few parents do make their children leave the house as soon as possible. Why do you think this happens?

3. In Paragraphs E and F, the authors state that a son may or may not accept a father's offer of a place in his business. Why might a son accept such an offer? Why might he reject it?

4. According to the authors' statements in Paragraph H, do American grandparents usually live with their sons and daughters, or somewhere else? In your country, where do grandparents live?

5. According to Paragraph H, how do some Americans feel about taking care of their elderly parents? Are changes regarding such care taking place in the United States?

6. In Paragraph K, the authors describe how grown children obtain the money they need to start their new life. Do they tend to ask family members or find an alternative source of financial support? How is this different from the financial practices in some ethnic groups?

7. As discussed in Paragraphs L and M, is it usual for both American parents to work? What are some reasons for both parents to work?

8. In your country, is there such a thing as the "commuter marriages" described in Paragraph P? How can such marriages survive? What insights do the authors offer?

9. Do you think the single-parent family described in Paragraph Q is "less" of a family? Why are there so many stresses on a single parent?

10. According to the authors' discussion in Paragraph U, is the American family dying? What is the authors' explanation?

Vocabulary Exercises

Vocabulary List

As you read the vocabulary list below, find two or three words you already know. Give their definitions.

Paragraph A	*Paragraph B*	*Paragraph C*
dimensions	indicative	esteem *estimar, apreciar*
		instill *to implant ideas or fee-lings into a peesons mind.*

Paragraph D	*Paragraph E*	*Paragraph F*
autonomy	spouses *cónyuges (hausband, wife)*	career
		deliberately
		self-reliant *independent "self-rilaiant"*

Paragraph G	*Paragraph H*	*Paragraph I*
treatment *=behaivor to another person*	child raising	distinguishing
peer *=equals*	retirement	communal *living as a group.*
indifference		
glorification		
alienated		

Paragraph J	*Paragraph K*	*Paragraph L*
ties *=close relationship*	residence	imposes
obligations	borrow	prescribed
	pool	

Paragraph M	*Paragraph N*	*Paragraph O*
professional	negotiating	equitable

Paragraph P	*Paragraph Q*	*Paragraph R*
commute *- viajar*	alimony *manutención*	approximately
	pago que se da cuando 1 pa-reja se divorcia.	

Paragraph S	*Paragraph T*	*Paragraph U*
blended family	regional	institution
constitute		accommodated
		morality
		shifts *trasladar, cambiar*

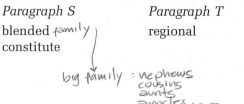

big family : nephews
cousins
aunts
uncles · · —

Phrases and Expressions

cut the (umbilical) cord [C]: become independent from one's
   parents
tied to mothers' apron strings [C]: very dependent on one's mother
look out for number one [C]: care only about one's self
stand on their own two feet [C]: be independent; self-sufficient
leave the nest [E]: become independent from one's family home; to
   leave home
social security [G]: government system of payment to retired people
senior citizen [G]: person over age sixty or sixty-five
nuclear family [H]: mother, father, children
extended family [H]: grandparents, aunts, uncles, cousins
breadwinner [L]: person who works to support the family
day care [N]: care for children when parents are working
dual career couples [O]: mother and father both have careers
commuter marriages [P]: husband and wife live in two separate
   locations because their places of work are geographically far apart
stretched to their limits [Q]: overly busy; pressured by many
   demands

A. Multiple Choice

Choose the word that *best* defines the italicized word.

1. In America, children are brought up to be *self-reliant.*   [F]
   a. happy
   b. independent
   c. strong
   d. handsome

2. The *elderly* are beginning to demand rights for themselves.   [G]
   a. parents
   b. couples
   c. aged
   d. children

3. Her *peers* were her worst critics.   [G]

    a. students

    (b.) equals

    c. teachers

    d. parents

4. The *glorification* of youth has created negative feelings toward the elderly.   [G]

    a. happiness

    b. education

    c. creation

    (d.) adoration

5. What should be done about our citizens' *indifference* to the international situation?   [G]

    (a.) lack of interest in

    b. lack of knowledge of

    c. lack of agreement about

    d. lack of understanding of

6. New students trying to meet friends on crowded campuses often feel *alienated*.   [G]

    a. ignorant

    b. awkward → torpe, tosco

    (c.) alone

    d. poor

7. *Communal* living works best for people who have similar beliefs.   [I]

    a. communistic

    b. individual

    c. independent

    (d.) group

8. Close family *ties* help children feel secure.   [J]

    a. homes

    b. bows

    c. relationships

    (d.) circles

9. Working parents have *obligations* to the family.   [J]
   a. needs
   b. responsibilities
   c. expectations
   d. compromises

10. Some parents work far from their homes, so they *commute* daily to get to their jobs.   [P]
   a. figure
   b. travel
   c. eat
   d. move

11. *Approximately* four out of five divorced couples eventually remarry other people.   [R]
   a. nearly
   b. near
   c. less than
   d. more than

12. The patterns of family relationships *shift* with every new generation.   [U]
   a. grow old
   b. change
   c. ripen
   d. tire

B. Definitions

Choose the correct word for the definition from the list below. Then fill in the blanks in the sentences following the definitions. *Note: You may have to change the grammatical form of the word used in the sentence.*

✓indicative [B]   ✓alimony [Q]
✓instill [C]   ✓constitute [S]
✓spouses [E]   ✓institution [U]
✓retirement [H]   ✓accommodated [U]
 distinguishing [I]

1. Definition: introduce or teach gradually ___instill___

   ___instilling___ good values in our children takes many years of patience.

2. Definition: withdrawal from work, usually due to old age

   ___retirement___

   My father ___retired___ when he was sixty-five years old and has been enjoying his free time.

3. Definition: formally establish; compose

   Exactly what ___constitutes___ a legal agreement?

4. Definition: setting apart; seeing ___distinguishing___

   Some criminals cannot ___distinguish___ right from wrong.

5. Definition: money paid in support to a divorced person by the former spouse ___alimony___

   She worked part time, collected ___alimony___, and eventually moved into a new apartment.

6. Definition: suggestive ___indicative___

   Her interesting questions ___indicated___ that she was enthusiastic about politics.

7. Definition: husbands or wives ___spouses___   "spowces"

   The company had a party and all the workers brought their ___spouses___.

8. Definition: an established practice, system, custom, or organization ___institution___

   Although the divorce rate is high, the ___institution___ of marriage still exists.

9. Definition: allowed for; accepted

   The hotel will try to ___accomodate___ you and the needs of your family.

C. Synonyms

Choose the appropriate synonym from the list to replace the italicized word, and rewrite each sentence. *Change tense, singular and plural usage, and part of speech when necessary.*

favorable regard · values
· geographical area   purposefully ~~determinado, intencional, provechoso.~~
✓aspects   ✓force
· independence   put together
✓professions   fair

1. The family structure can *impose* set roles upon both parents and children.   [L]

   The family structure can FORCE roles upon both parents and children

2. Some mothers manage to balance their time effectively between their *careers* and their families.   [F]

   Some mothers manage to balance their time effectively between their PROFESSIONS and their families

3. In a different chapter, you read that nonverbal communication is one of the "hidden" *dimensions* of language.   [A]

   In a different chapter, you read that nonverbal communication is one of the "hidden" ASPECTS of language

4. The two business partners worked for hours to reach an *equitable* arrangement.   [O]

   The two business partners worked for hours to reach a FAIR arrangement

5. I cannot believe that my friend would want to hurt my feelings *deliberately*.   [F]

   I cannot believe that my friend would want to hurt my feelings PURPOSEFULLY

6. If you hold your hero in high *esteem*, it means that you admire him very much.   [C]

   If you hold your hero in high FAVORABLE REGARD, it means that you admire him very much

7. In America, people can accomplish many things if they know how to *pool* their resources.   [K]

   In America, people can accomplish many things if they know how to PUT TOGETHER their resources

8. Many young people in America try to assert their *autonomy* by going against their parents' advice.   [D]

   Many young people in America try to assert their INDEPENDENCE by going against their parent's advice

9. Some people feel that parents no longer teach *morality* to their children.   [U]

   Some people feel that parents no longer teach VALUES to their children

10. What *region* of the United States is your favorite?

    What GEOGRAPHICAL AREA of the U.S. is your favorite?

D. Definitions in Context

Try to guess the meaning of the italicized word by looking at its context in the sentence. Write a definition in the space provided. Check your dictionary only after you have tried to determine the meaning yourself.

1. *Child raising* can be a wonderful experience for parents, if they are patient and like to see children grow. [H] → *to bring up (only for children)*

   It's the evolution when a child is growing up to be a responsable adult (take care) of your kid

2. Many college students live in a *residence* hall, where they have a room and can get three meals every day. [K]

   apartment, dormitory, place where you live

3. If I *borrow* your cassette tape tonight and take it home with me, I promise to return it tomorrow. [K]

   to take something and then return it (take temporaly)

4. Some companies have *prescribed* rules for proper dress and behavior. [L] *prescritas*

   to advise, to give a specifil recomendation, define rules.

5. I want to take a class that relates to my work, so please give me the list of *professional* classes. [M]

   classes with a high level, related with job or career

6. Even though many countries have already started to make an effort, it will take years to *negotiate* a plan for world peace. [N]

   arrangement, treat, discuss and figured out a problem

7. A family may be a *blended* one in which both parents have been divorced and have remarried, bringing both sets of children into the family. [S]

   combined, mixed up together

8. Society's *treatment* of the aged reflects its values and attitudes toward the elderly. [G] → *the way to act (trato)*

   arrangement, to deal with a person,

E. Phrases and Expressions

Which statement *best* conveys the meaning of the *italicized* words?

1. To *cut the cord* is: [C]
   a. to become independent of one's parents.
   b. to cut a piece of string.
   c. an expression used by electricians.

2. Children who are *tied to their mothers' apron strings*:   [C]
   a. are caught in their mothers' aprons. mandil
   b. must always wear an apron when they eat.
   c. are very dependent on their mothers.

3. To *leave the nest* means to: [E]
   a. go to the nest of new parents.
   b. try to be like a bird and fly.
   c. leave home permanently.

4. *Senior citizens* are: [G]
   a. people over forty-five years of age.
   b. only older grandparents.
   c. usually over the age of sixty.

5. *Social Security* can be obtained by: [G]
   a. retired and disabled people.
   b. working parents without children.
   c. children without parents. ⋅ also works

6. The term *nuclear family* refers to the: [H, I]
   a. mother, father, sisters, and brothers.
   b. family of one's spouse.
   c. family members who protect you from nuclear power plants.

7. The *extended family* includes: [H, I]
   a. grandparents, aunts, and uncles.
   b. cousins, nephews, and nieces.
   c. both (a) and (b).

8. A *breadwinner* is a: [L]
   a. person who supports the family financially.
   b. person who puts the bread on the table.
   c. mother who wins a bread-baking contest.

Conversational Activities

A. Disciplining Children

Watching the way parents interact with and discipline their children can give insight into the cultural behavior of older children and adults. Just as there are cultural styles of communication, there are styles of disciplining children across cultures. Read the article[8] below about an American pattern of discipline and then discuss the questions that follow.

Disciplining children
Parents say spanking OK

More than half of America's adults believe parents should spank their children when they think it's necessary, despite almost uniform agreement among child-development specialists that spanking is an inappropriate and ineffective form of discipline.

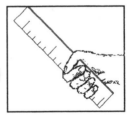

A Working Mothers magazine poll of 7,225 adults and 2,599 children found that the most common form of discipline is taking away privileges, followed by spanking and reasoning with the child. Forty-two percent of the adults said taking away privileges is the most effective discipline, compared with 13 percent who said spanking is.

Men are more likely to favor spanking than women and less likely to feel guilty about it, the poll indicated. Also, parents who live in the South and Midwest tend to favor spanking more than those who live in the West and Northeast.

The poll was conducted at Walt Disney World Epcot Center in Florida.

" Spare the rod, spoil the child "

not use
not kill
stick
palo
consentido
mimado

Discuss

1. Do you think spanking is an effective form of disciplining children? Do your beliefs reflect cultural beliefs?

2. What are other ways that children can be disciplined?

3. There used to be a common belief in the United States that "children should be seen and not heard." (There are still some American parents who follow this advice, but they are not the majority.) What is your reaction to this statement? Does your response reflect a cultural belief?

4. Have you observed American parents interacting with their children? If so, have you noticed any cross-cultural differences? Explain.

juventud

B. A Case Study: **Youth** and the Family

The following story[9] tells of an incident in an American family in which a daughter goes against her parents' wishes. Meida, a foreign student from India, observes the situation and is confused about what is happening. Read the story aloud, and then discuss the questions that follow.

> Meida: Foreign student
>
> Carol: Meida's American friend
>
> Dr. Turner: Carol's father
>
> Mrs. Turner: Carol's mother

Meida has been invited to the Turners' home for dinner. She is sitting at the table, and is enjoying dinner and conversation with the rest of the family. During dinner, the phone rings and Carol's younger brother answers it. The following conversation takes place:

> *Carol's Brother:* Carol, it's Bill.
>
> *Mrs. Turner (surprised):* Bill? I thought you weren't seeing him any more, Carol.

Without replying, Carol leaves the room to answer the phone. When she returns, she silently continues her dinner.

> *Dr. Turner:* Carol, was it Bill?
>
> *Carol:* Yes.

Dr. Turner:	Are you still seeing him, even though we told you we didn't approve?
Carol (angrily):	Do I have to tell you everything? Listen, Dad, I know Bill doesn't have a college education, but he is working for his brother in a construction company. He's trying to earn enough money to return to school. You always say that you respect hard-working people. Why shouldn't I see him any more?
Dr. Turner (softly but seriously):	I hope you're not serious about Bill, Carol. He promised to stay in college, but he dropped out two times. Do you want to marry someone whose personality you'll have to change?
Mrs. Turner:	Carol, Bill is different from us. We're only saying this because we love you. Bill just isn't your kind.
Carol (furious):	What do you mean, "my kind"? He's a human being! Just because he comes from a family that has less money than we do? What kind of democracy do you believe in? Everyone is supposed to be equal. He and his family are just as good as we are.

By now, Carol is shouting loudly. Meida is feeling embarrassed and stares at her plate.

Carol's Brother:	Come on, Mom and Dad. Bill's a nice guy.
Carol:	Just because his parents are farmers who work with their hands and you are professors who work with your heads. What difference does that make?
Mrs. Turner:	Carol, we're very disappointed in you. After all, we know what is best for you.

Suddenly Carol gets up, takes Meida's arm, and pulls her to the door.

Carol:	Come on, Meida, Let's go to my room and study.

Carol and Meida quickly walk out. Meida tries to say to Carol's parents that she is sorry, but Carol pulls her away.

Discuss

1. What were the problems between Carol and her parents?
2. Who do you think was right?
3. Explain your answer.

After discussing the incident, consider the following questions. Discuss them in small groups, or write a short composition.

1. Could this situation have occurred in your family? Why or why not?
2. Would your family disagree or argue in front of guests? Do you think any members of Carol's family were rude?
3. Does a "generation gap" exist in your culture? That is, are there usually differences between the way young people and their parents think?

C. Common Problems Among Family Members

The following are a few examples of situations that might occur among family members in the United States. In pairs or small groups, discuss the situations, and answer the questions that follow.

1. The son or daughter does poorly in school.
2. The son or daughter elopes (secretly runs away to get married).
3. The son wants to live with his fiancée before getting married (or the daughter with her fiancé).
4. The parents of married daughters and sons try to tell their children how to live.
5. Eight months after her husband has died, the widowed mother of grown children announces that she is going to remarry.
6. The grown children of very ill parents feel that they have to move their parents into a nursing home. The parents refuse to cooperate.

Discuss

1. How do these problems compare with problems among family members in your country?

2. How would your family deal with these types of problems?

3. Do you feel the sex of a child would make a difference in the way an American family would handle any of the above situations? If so, which ones?

4. If these problems are not typical in your country, what other kinds of family problems might occur?

D. Open Role-Playing

Divide, into small groups with members of the same culture (if possible),* and complete the following exercise.

1. First think of common problems that occur among family members in your country. Try to choose a problem that illustrates cultural beliefs or values.

2. Assign roles to group members (i.e., choose someone to play the part of the mother, father, son, etc.). Practice the role-playing.

3. Act out the role-playing in front of the rest of the class.

Discuss

1. Is the problem you selected to act out a typical one in your country?

2. Could it happen in any country?

E. Division of Labor

On p. 200 is a list of common family activities and duties. Who in your family would be responsible for these activities? Check whether it would be the father, the mother, the child, the grandparent (or other relatives), or a combination of any of these.

Discuss

Which, if any, of the familial roles are changing?

---

*If all class members are from the same country, choose several problems common in that country.

	Father	Mother	Child	Grand-parent*
Financial				
Keeping family accounts				
Shopping for food				
Cooking dinner				
Housekeeping				
Home repairs				
Punishing the children				
Disciplining the children				
Major family decisions				
Buying a car				
Moving to a new home				
Children's education				
Selecting a child's spouse				
Vacations				
Divorce				

* or other relative

F. Cross-Cultural Questions

Answer the following questions about your own culture, and then discuss cross-cultural similarities and differences.

1. What is your idea of the "ideal" family? Describe the roles of the family members and the beliefs that unite a family.

2. How would children be rewarded and punished within the "ideal" family?

3. What kinds of activities does your family do together for fun? Are these activities done with the nuclear family or with the extended family and friends?

4. Do external factors such as politics, technology, or the media affect the way families behave? If so, how? (For example, the average American child watches two to four hours of television a day.)

5. Is the family unit changing in any way in your country (for example, number of children, education level of family members, etc.)?

Cultural Notes

1. Terms used to address members of the family include the following:

Nuclear Family

Parents:	Folks
Father:	Dad, Daddy, Pa, Papa
Mother:	Mom, Mommy, Ma, Mamma
Children:	Kids

Extended Family

Grandparents:	Grandmother, Grandma, Grandfather, Grandpa
Uncle:	first name or Uncle + first name
Aunt:	first name or Aunt + first name, Auntie
Cousins, nephews, nieces:	first names

2. Other terms for family members (not terms of address):

In-laws:	mother-in-law, father-in-law, brother-in-law, sister-in-law
Stepfamilies:	stepparents, stepsister, stepbrother, half-brother, half-sister

3. Occasionally, children call their parents by their first names. This is often the case with stepparents. Parents usually address their children by their first names, nicknames, or occasionally by their first and middle names. Mothers- and fathers-in-law are often called by their first names, but are sometimes referred to as "Mother" and "Father."

4. If you are attending a family gathering and would like to know what the familial relationship is between one member and another, you may ask, "How are you related?"

5. The following are some of the activities that families share in the United States:

   a. birthdays

   b. annual reunions

   c. religious and secular holidays (Thanksgiving, Christmas, Easter, Passover, etc.)

   d. religious ceremonies (baptism, confirmation, bar/bat mitzvah)

   e. weddings

   f. wedding anniversaries

   g. leisure activities (picnics, camping, dining out, movies)

6. The following are legal arrangements that relate to the family:

   a. *Marriage*: Usually the decision to marry is based on a mutual agreement between the man and the woman. Parents may or may not be asked to give their permission. The marriage ceremony may be a simple visit to city hall, where marriage vows are exchanged and papers are signed, or it can be an elaborate religious/festive celebration. There are numerous alternatives to the traditional wedding ceremony.

   b. *Adoption*: The practice of adopting children exists for parents who cannot have their own children, for parents who decide by choice not to have their own children, and for single parents (although it is difficult for them to adopt). This practice is not considered unusual or negative in the American culture.

   c. *Separation*: Couples who do not wish to get divorced may decide by mutual agreement to separate; in this case, they are still legally married. Couples who have filed for divorce are separated until the divorce is finalized.

   d. *Divorce*: Divorces can be obtained easily in most American states. Either husbands or wives can apply for divorce. Bases for divorce can be as diverse as mutual agreement of "incompatibility" to accusations of brutal treatment. There is usually a minimal waiting time for remarriage. Child support payments, alimony, and the division of property are usually arranged by the courts or by mutual agreement between the husband and wife.

7. Some institutions in society are changing in order to help the family maintain close bonds. In some jobs, new mothers are given "maternity leave" that allows them up to six months off with pay. Recently, some employers have been granting short "paternity leave" to men whose wives have delivered babies. In this way the

man can take care of the house and child as the woman is recovering from delivery.

Supplementary Vocabulary and Phrases

matriarchal	juvenile	ancestors
patriarchal	family income	aged
offspring	lower class family	family tree
puberty	middle class family	marriage license
adolescence	upper class family	bride
		groom

7

Education: Values and Expectations

"For a young student who comes from a small place, the American college or university is like a Big Mac.* It's too big to eat it all."

International Student in the United States

Pre-Reading Discussion

1. In your opinion, what aspects of the American educational system are most difficult for foreign students and immigrants? Base your answer on your experience or the experience of people you know.

2. What are your expectations of professors and instructors? Should they be more than teachers? For example, should they also be counselors, friends, or advisers?

3. In your culture, is "peer-teaching" common? That is, do students ever teach each other?

*A very large McDonald's hamburger

Pre-Reading Vocabulary

1. Definition

   student participation: active involvement of a student in the learning process, especially in the classroom. In the United States, student participation is not only accepted but expected.

   Discussion: Do teachers encourage student participation in your culture, or does the teacher dominate the class while students remain quiet? If students are expected to remain quiet, are they given any opportunities to communicate with the teacher? Explain.

2. Definition

   honor system: the demand that a student be honest in all areas of schoolwork; no cheating of any kind is allowed.

   Discussion: In other schools that you have attended, what happened when a student was caught cheating? In your opinion, should students be punished strictly if they share answers on tests or on schoolwork?

3. Definitions

   a. **cooperative student relationships**: relationships characterized by students' willingness to work together as a team, and to share knowledge and information.

   b. **competitive student relationships**: relationships characterized by students' desire to work alone, and not to share knowledge and information with others.

   Discussion: In your culture, are relationships between students generally cooperative or competitive? What are the advantages and disadvantages of working in groups and working alone? What is your preference?

Skimming: For General Information

To get the general idea of the reading that follows:

1. Read the titles and headings of the sections.
2. Read the first and last paragraphs of the reading.

From your skimming, answer the following:

1. Are classroom expectations the same in every country?
2. Where is the answer to this question found?

Scanning: For Specific Information

To find specific information in the reading, look for clues such as certain words and numbers. Scan the reading to find the answers to the following:

1. In which paragraph have the authors listed ways to manage stress? What are three of the ways?
2. What is "peer counseling"? In which paragraph did you find the definition?

Reading Text

Education: Values and Expectations

[A] International students and immigrants attending schools in the United States can experience multiple "culture shocks." Students from abroad, accustomed to their countries' educational expectations, must adapt to new classroom °norms in a foreign educational institu-
5   tion. In some other countries, students must °humbly obey their teachers' directions and remain absolutely silent during a class. Yet in other cultures, students are allowed to criticize or even °contradict their teachers. In one country, a prayer in the classroom may be acceptable, while in another it may be °forbidden. Cultural differ-
10   ences as well as the experience of being a newcomer account for some of the adjustment problems that non-native-born students expe-

rience. At the same time, a °diverse student population on campuses helps some Americans appreciate that there are different habits, customs, and attitudes, and that the "American way" is not the only way.

15

Diversity in Higher Education

[B] Young students, middle-aged students, and senior citizens who wish to continue or extend their education have a variety of institutions of higher learning from which to choose in the United States. Some communities have adult schools as well as two-year colleges (which

5 are also called "junior colleges" and "community colleges"). Not all students pursue a specific degree as their goal. They may simply want to receive specific vocational training that will assist them in their jobs (e.g., computer programming or language instruction). Alternatively, if they have °substantial °leisure time (as many retired

10 people do), they may take courses to pursue interests for which they were too busy when they were younger. Many four-year colleges or universities also have graduate programs for people seeking advanced degrees.

[C] There is a saying in the American culture that "you are never too old to learn." Increasingly, one sees older and younger people studying together in American institutions of higher learning. Women are encouraged to gain new skills to be able to enter the job market

5 after their children are grown. Other people change careers, which often requires additional education. Institutions are attempting to meet the diverse needs and goals of these students.

Active Participation

[D] Student °participation in the classroom is not only accepted but also expected in most subjects. Some instructors and professors* base part of the student's grade on oral participation. Courses are often organized around classroom discussions, student questions, and informal

5 lectures, although large classes can involve formal lectures during which the student has a passive role.

[E] In a small percentage of the more informal classes, students may even decide the topics for study and choose °appropriate books and articles. Allowing the student to take the lead in this manner is confusing for people in many other cultures. A Japanese student was

5 shocked when her professor told the class, "I want you to come up

---

*The term "instructor" is usually used for teachers in adult schools (sometimes referred to as "night schools"), and junior, city, and community colleges. The term "professor" is usually used for teachers in four-year colleges and universities. In this reading, "instructor" and "professor" are used interchangeably.

with an outline for the course and a list of books to read." She felt
that the professor was not doing his job and was totally °incompetent.
The student knew that the professor had always received extremely
good evaluations from his students in previous courses. However, she
10 could not bring herself to accept his authority when he treated his
students as if they were equals and as if they possessed as much
knowledge as he had.

[F]   In some courses (mainly graduate seminars), the teacher has
only a °managerial role and the students do the actual teaching
through discussions and presentations. It is common for instructors
to guide students to take the °initiative and to be responsible for their
5   learning. Especially students pursuing advanced degrees are expected
to be actively involved in their own education. They must be ready to
critique theories, formulate models, and interact with the professor.
Students who do not ask questions and do not bring up their own
ideas may appear to be uninterested in the course.

[G]   A professor's teaching style is another factor that determines the
degree and type of student participation. Some instructors and professors prefer to guide the class without dominating it. Many encourage students to question and challenge their ideas. Students who con-
5   tradict teachers must be prepared to defend their positions. In

general, confident and experienced instructors do not object to students who disagree with them.

[H]   Instruction in science and mathematics is usually more traditional, with teachers presenting formal lectures and students taking notes. However, the educational trends that have influenced the teaching of the humanities and social sciences have also affected
5   mathematics and the "hard sciences." Students may be asked to solve problems in groups or to °design projects. Classes that are considered applied rather than °theoretical °stress such °"hands-on" involvement.

The Teacher-Student Relationship

[I]   Many teachers believe that the responsibility for learning lies with the student. If a reading assignment is given, instructors expect students to be familiar with the information in the reading, even if they do not discuss it in class or give an examination. The ideal student is
5   considered to be one who is °motivated to learn for the sake of learning, not the one who is interested only in getting high grades. Unlike in some other countries, in the United States courses are not usually designed merely for students to pass exams. A teacher does not respect a student who only comes to class on the last day to take an
10   exam.

[J]   Many instructors hold a belief, reflecting cultural values, that an informal, relaxed classroom environment is °conducive to learning and °innovation. It is common for students to have easygoing and friendly relationships with their professors. The casual professor is
5   not necessarily a poor one and is still respected by students. Although students may be in a °subordinate position, some instructors try to treat them as equals within the limits of the teacher-

student relationship (°egalitarianism and informality are characteristic American traits).

[K]   Professors and instructors may establish social relationships with students outside of the classroom, but in the classroom they °maintain the teacher's role. A professor may go out for coffee with a student, but still expects the student to meet °deadlines and study for
5   exams. The teacher may give extra attention outside of class to a student in need of help, but probably will not °treat the person differently when evaluating schoolwork.

[L]   Professors have several roles in relation to students: they may be counselors and friends as well as teachers. Students must realize that when a professor's role changes, they must appropriately adapt their behavior and attitudes. An American professor and his Middle
5   Eastern graduate student became friends, but the student was not able to adjust to the different roles the professor had to play. When the student would come to the office and sit for one to two hours at a time, the professor became °resentful of what he perceived was an intrusion. However, the student did not intend to anger his professor/friend. The student had a more relaxed attitude about time that
10 was tied to his culture, and he, unlike the professor, did not separate work (or study) from socializing. The American professor °compart-

mentalized his work and social time. The distinction for the student was unclear.

Trust, Honesty, and the Honor System

[M]   Trust is an important expectation in American education. The °"honor system," imposed by the teacher and the school, demands that the student be honest in all areas of schoolwork. °Violation of the honor system can result in failing a course, having a permanent
5   record of the violation in the student's files, and even being °suspended or °expelled from the university. Many students are also aware that they can °jeopardize their rapport with fellow students if they are dishonest. Students who cheat may lose the respect of other students, particularly those who study for exams and work indepen-
10   dently. Some instructors leave their classrooms when students are taking an exam. They may or may not say, "I expect you all to abide by the honor system" (which means, "Don't cheat!"). Even if the words are not stated, the student is expected to work alone and not share answers.

[N]   In one midwestern university handbook,[1] the following behaviors are listed as examples of academic dishonesty:

"pleiycraism"

- °*Plagiarism*—Using other people's work and submitting it as your own without citing the source. *("piratear" ideas de libros ...)*
- °*Cheating*—This includes tests, take-home exams, and papers submitted for credit.
- °*Fabrication*—Reporting false or inaccurate data. *(invent facts)*
- *Aiding ... dishonesty*—Knowingly providing information to another student that would be used dishonestly. *(dejar copiar)*
- °*Falsification* of records and official documents—This includes forging signatures or falsifying information on academic documents.

[O]   College officials take these rules seriously and punish accordingly. (Although some American students do try to cheat, they know what the consequences are.) Plagiarism, or presenting another's ideas (either in written or oral form) as one's own, is a concept tied to cul-
5   tural beliefs. Americans believe in respect for other people's property, and this includes their ideas as well as their research. The words and ideas of academicians, scholars, and researchers are considered private property. If others' research and ideas are to be used in someone else's work, they must be acknowledged by a citation (a written refer-
10   ence indicating the source of the material). Sometimes, it is necessary to obtain written permission to use an extended piece of information (or ideas) in a book or article to be published. When international students are °accused of plagiarism, it may be that they omitted the citation out of ignorance and not because of dishonesty. In the academic
15   world, Americans consider the lack of citation as °tantamount to a "stolen" idea. Many students from other countries do not share similar ideas about private property, especially private property in the form of ideas or research. Still, they have to adapt to the rules of their college or university.

[P]   Students from countries where °"beating the system" is a survival technique have to adjust to the fact that in the United States any kind of falsification of official school documents is considered dishonest and is punishable. In an attempt to "beat the system," several
5   Eastern European students were expelled from their college after it was discovered that they had given false information about their prior schooling on their applications for admission. Their attempt to take advantage of the system in order to better themselves may have been a natural response to having struggled in a society with many
10   °bureaucratic barriers. Nevertheless, the American university °administrators could not excuse this kind of dishonest behavior, despite the students' cultural background.

Competition and Grading

[Q] Relationships between students in the classroom can be either °cooperative or °competitive. In programs or courses where a degree is not being pursued or where grades are not given, there is usually a friendly exchange of information among students. Likewise, when
5   courses are taken for credit only (i.e., the students will be graded either "pass" or "fail" only), students are willing to share notes and be helpful toward each other. However, in some courses, an individual's grades are °calculated in relation to others' scores. Therefore, in classes where such a grading "curve"* is used, students may be
10 °reluctant to share lecture notes or other information for fear that their own grades will suffer.

[R]   There are other reasons for the presence of competition among students. A high grade-point average (GPA)† is needed for entrance to superior graduate schools. Students feel pressure to achieve high grades when there are relatively few openings in graduate programs.
5   In addition, when facing a competitive job market, graduates may be hired largely on the basis of their grades and faculty recommendations. Generally, American students are fairly grade conscious and often look for ways to improve their GPA. Some instructors give students opportunities to do extra-credit assignments.

*For an explanation of the grading curve, see p. 236.
†For an explanation of the GPA, see p. 236.

[S]   Occasionally, students disagree with the grade they have been given by their instructor. In this °circumstance, if evidence is shown that the grade (whether for an exam or for the entire course) does not reflect the students' work, they may approach their professor with
5   their objection and ask for a change in the grade. It is extremely important that students be polite and respectful (yet assertive) and not express anger.

Student Stress and Coping

[T]   Younger students sometimes have emotional problems in their educational environment. The stress of taking exams and of meeting deadlines can cause difficulty for those not used to responsibility and intense work. On the other hand, older students with children or
5   with experience in jobs or the military adapt to pressure and stress more easily. A student who is also the parent of three children, for example, knows that grades, exams, and reports are not the most important aspects of life. Older students are also less likely to be °intimidated by instructors or professors.

[U]   When some American students find it difficult to cope and have excessive stress, they may seek counseling (usually with college counselors or psychologists). Many schools offer °"peer counseling" in which students with experience actually advise other students.
5 Younger students living away from home for the first time may not know how to handle their newly found freedom and responsibility, and may prefer to talk to someone close in age who has had similar problems. For many international students and new immigrants in the United States, counseling, whether by peers or older psycholo-
10 gists, is not culturally comfortable. (In many cultures, one does not talk to strangers about personal problems.) There are certain things that students can do on their own to cope with problems. In one university handbook, students are advised to try to manage stress by doing the following:[2]

1. Exercise regularly.
2. Make certain you get enough sleep during stressful times.
3. Learn to relax your body.
4. Set priorities; think about one concern at a time.

5. Learn to accept what you cannot change.

6. Learn to say, "No" (i.e., do not let yourself be persuaded to do things you do not want to do).

7. Talk it out: share your stress with someone you trust.

8. Know your limits.

9. Take care of yourself.

10. Make time for fun.

11. Avoid self-medication with drugs and alcohol.

12. Develop a support network of friends.

International and Immigrant Students in the United States

[V] There are some °predictable problem areas for international students and immigrants studying in the United States. Making friends is a challenge (this is also true for some American students). Many colleges and universities offer a variety of student clubs and organiza-
5 tions where both foreign-born and American students have a greater chance of meeting people with shared interests. Information about these °extracurricular activities is often posted in the student center and listed in the student newspaper. Sometimes foreign students and immigrant students find Americans to be °"cliquish." (Americans
10 find some non–U.S.-born students to be cliquish as well.) If people feel excluded from the social aspects of American college life, they should actively seek people with shared interests. It is unlikely that students will make friends just by passing people in the hallways.

[W] Foreign or immigrant students may be disoriented during the first few weeks at a new school because they do not understand the system and are not willing to ask questions. Many students do not take advantage of the numerous services offered on campus that
5 assist students in developing new skills and social groups. Some colleges offer students tutorial support in such subjects as writing, language study, computer skills, and other basic subjects.* Students who appear to be most successful in °"learning the ropes" are those who take the initiative to ask questions, locate °resources, and experience
10 new social situations.

[X] The American classroom is governed by numerous culturally dictated attitudes and expectations. For example, educational practices such as the honor system and student participation indicate a respect for individual responsibility and independence. Foreign and

*For further explanation of types of assistance offered on some campuses, see p. 237.

5   immigrant students should anticipate that cross-cultural misunderstandings may arise as a result of differences. Having an awareness of cultural differences and flexibility with regard to one's own expectations and behavior are important factors in °enhancing successful learning.

Comprehension Questions*

1. According to the authors, international students and immigrants attending schools in the United States may experience: [A]

   a. multiple culture shocks.

   b. a large culture shock.

   c. no adjustment problems.

That there are different habits, customs, attitudes. And the 'America way' isn't the only way .

2. According to the authors, what does the diverse student population on campuses help some Americans to appreciate?   [A]

3. If students are not going to school to get a degree, why might they be taking classes?   [B] *① to receive a specific vocational training ② just for interest*

4. There is a belief in the American culture regarding ages at which people can learn. According to this belief, when are people too old to learn?   [C] *"You're never too old to learn"*

5. "Student participation in the classroom is not only accepted but also expected in most subjects." However, this is not generally true in: [D]

   a. small classes that have many discussions.

   b. informal lecture courses.

   c. large classes with formal lectures.

6. Students pursuing advanced degrees are expected to: [F]

   a. critique the professor.

   b. formulate models.

   c. critique theories.

   d. both (b) and (c).

7. Educational trends that have influenced teaching in the humanities and social sciences as well as in mathematics and the "hard sciences" have been responsible for what kind of classroom activities?   [H] *Theorical, stress such , hands-on , involvment.*

*The capital letters in brackets refer to the corresponding paragraphs in the reading.

8. Many teachers believe that the responsibility for learning:　[I]

    a. lies with the teacher.

    b. belongs to the school.

    (c.) lies with the student.

9. What kind of classroom environment is believed to help a student learn?　[J]

    a. formal and structured

    (b.) informal and relaxed

    c. easy and casual

10. According to the authors, will a teacher who socializes with students outside of class evaluate them differently? In other words, will teachers do favors for their students with whom they have a close relationship?　[K] *No, the teachear maintain his role. The teacher may give extra attention but he'll not treat the person differently in the evaluations.*

11. What might be a result of a violation of the honor system?　[M]

    a. a student's failing a course

    b. a permanent record of the violation in a student's file

    c. suspension or expulsion from the university

    (d.) all of the above

12. What are three examples of academic dishonesty?　[N]
Plagiarism, Cheating & Fabrication.

13. When international students are accused of plagiarism, is it always because of dishonesty? What is another possible cause that the authors give?　[O] *The students may be ignorant about the system, but not necessarily dishonest*

14. Why might students be hesitant to share lecture notes or other information with their fellow students?　[Q] *'cause they feel that their own grades will suffer*

15. Give two specific reasons that a high grade-point average is important to some students.　[Q, R] *① is needed for entrance to superior graduate school. ② they feel pressure to achieve high grades*

16. According to the authors, who might adapt better to the stress of academic life?　[T]

    (a.) older students

    b. younger students

    c. new students

17. Why do some students who find it difficult to cope prefer peer counseling to counseling with a school psychologist?　[U] *They prefer to talk to somone close in age who has had the same problems*

18. Is it likely that students will make friends just by passing people in the hallways at school?　[V]
No, it isn't. There are a lot of extracurricular activities

19. According to the authors, why might foreign or immigrant students be disoriented during the first few weeks at a new school? [W] *They don't understand the system & are not willing to ask questions*

20. What American values does the university reflect?   [X]

   a. democracy, socialism, and authoritarianism

   b. absolute respect, formality, and tradition

   c. individual responsibility and independence

Discussion Questions

Students should prepare these before class discussion.

1. What is the main theme of this reading?

   a. academic success in schools in the United States

   b. behavior, attitudes, and values found in the American educational system

   c. competition in American society

2. The authors say in Paragraph A that international students and immigrants must adapt to new classroom norms when they study in a foreign educational institution. How have you had to adapt to culturally different classroom norms? How would American students have to adapt to educational norms in classes in your culture?

3. In Paragraph C, the authors say that older and younger people study together in America. Does this occur in your culture? Have you ever been in an educational setting with much older or much younger students?

4. Student participation is expected in most subjects, according to the authors' discussion in Paragraph E. Did you ever have a class in which the students did most of the talking? If so, was this classroom style comfortable for you?

5. In Paragraph E, the authors state that it is confusing for some students to take the lead in deciding upon topics and choosing books and articles for their classes. Why is this so?

6. In Paragraph F, the authors say that a certain type of student is expected to be actively involved in his or her own education. What type of student is this? What behavior would make a professor think that this type of student was uninterested in learning?

7. In Paragraph G, the authors discuss the fact that many professors encourage their students to challenge their ideas. If a student makes such a challenge, what must the student be prepared to do? Do experienced teachers become insulted by students who disagree with them? Discuss.

8. Describe the "ideal" student discussed by the authors in Paragraph I. In your opinion, what else makes an ideal student? What makes an ideal teacher?

9. According to the authors' statements in Paragraph J, how do egalitarianism and informality relate to the way students and teachers interact?

10. According to the authors' discussion in Paragraph K, are the roles that professors establish outside the classroom the same as the roles that they maintain inside the classroom? Have you ever become friends with a teacher? Were there any conflicts in the relationship because you were also a student?

11. The authors say in Paragraph M that the "honor system" is imposed by the teacher and the school. In your culture, do university students expect to be trusted? Explain.

12. Reread the list of examples of academic dishonesty in Paragraph N. Are these acts considered dishonest in your country of origin? What are the consequences of breaking these rules in your own country?

13. How can cultural background affect the way that students understand academic rules? Give specific examples, using the discussion in Paragraphs N, O, and P as your guide.

14. In Paragraph S, the authors say that when students disagree with their professors about a grade, they can approach them in an attempt to change the grade. Is this true in your culture? Would you feel comfortable asking a professor to change your grade?

15. In Paragraph T, the authors say that younger students especially may tend to have emotional problems in their educational environment. What is an aspect of the academic atmosphere that may cause some difficulty? Give three specific tips you would offer to a new international student or immigrant at an American university or college.

16. In Paragraph U, the authors suggest counseling for American students who find it difficult to cope with academic stress. In your culture, if students feel overwhelmed by the demands of a university, what do they do? Do they turn to friends, seek counseling, talk with their professors, or go to their families? Explain.

17. Reread the list of stress management techniques in Paragraph U. Which do you think are the most and least helpful? Choose two of each and discuss.

18. What are some ways that the authors suggest in Paragraph V for making friends in the university setting? From your observations of Americans, have you noticed that they use these ways of making friends?

19. According to the authors in Paragraph W, which students appear to be most successful in "learning the ropes"? Do these skills rely on language ability only? Discuss.

20. In Paragraph X, the authors say that having both an awareness of cultural differences and flexibility in one's expectations and behavior are important factors in successful learning. Do you agree? Are other elements involved in successful learning? If so, which would you add?

Vocabulary Exercises

Vocabulary List

As you read the vocabulary list below, find two or three words you already know. Give their definitions.

Paragraph A	*Paragraph B*	*Paragraph D*
norms	substantial	participation
humbly humilde	leisure tiempo libre ocio	
contradict		
forbidden prohibir		
diverse		

Paragraph E	*Paragraph F*	*Paragraph H*
appropriate	managerial administrativo	design
incompetent	initiative iniciativa	theoretical
		stress

Paragraph I	*Paragraph J*	*Paragraph K*
motivated	conducive	maintain
	innovation	deadlines
	subordinate	treat
	egalitarianism	

Paragraph L	*Paragraph M*	*Paragraph N*
resentful	violation	plagiarism
compartmentalized	suspended	cheating
	expelled *expulsar*	fabrication
	jeopardize *arriesgar*	falsification

Paragraph O	*Paragraph P*	*Paragraph Q*
accused	bureaucratic	cooperative
tantamount *equivalente*	administrators	competitive
		calculated
		reluctant

Paragraph S	*Paragraph T*	*Paragraph V*
circumstance	intimidated	predictable
		extracurricular
		cliquish *exclusivista*

Paragraph W	*Paragraph X*
resources	enhancing *mejorar*

Phrases and Expressions

hands-on [H]: applied; direct involvement

honor system [M]: system whereby students are trusted by their professors and assumed to be honest

beat the system [P]: use dishonest ways to succeed

peer counseling [U]: counseling or advice given from student to student

learning the ropes [W]: learning the system

A. Multiple Choice

Choose the word that *best* defines the *italicized* word.

1. Her *leisure* activities include reading and writing letters to her friends.   [B]
   a. free time
   b. work
   c. unpaid
   d. last

2. I could get a *substantial* amount done tonight if I work for a couple of hours. [B]

   a. little

   b. large

   c. adequate

   d. marginal

3. It is *appropriate* to make an appointment with a professor before going to his office. [E]

   a. incorrect

   b. believed

   c. acceptable and expected

   d. daring

4. It is important for students to take the *initiative* and be responsible for their own learning. [F]

   a. first step

   b. defensive position

   c. easy way out

   d. passive role

5. The student was not *motivated* to perform well in her classes. [I]

   a. encouraged

   b. stimulated

   c. aware

   d. asked

6. Many students are *resentful* of too many rules because they feel as though they are being treated as children. [L]

   a. happy with

   b. bored by

   c. angry about

   d. concerned with

7. The professor *compartmentalized* her work and social time, and thus was able to enjoy both. [L]

   a. combined

   b. left out

   c. determined

   d. separated

8. Anyone who is *accused* of a crime in the United States has a right to a lawyer.   [O]

(a) charged with

b. told

c. escaped

d. freed

9. Americans feel that using someone's words in a research paper without referencing them is *tantamount* to stealing.   [O]

a. necessary

b. unbelievable

c. acceptable

(d) equivalent

10. To understand another person's *circumstance*, it is important to listen carefully to his or her story.   [S]

(a) situation

b. history

c. excuse

d. idea

11. There are many ways of *enhancing* one's study skills: begin with setting manageable goals.   [X]

(a) improving

b. assisting

c. losing

d. combining

B. Matching

Match the words with their definitions. Place the letter of the definition in the space next to the word.

"mentiroso"

__d__ jeopardize	a.	the act of being deceitful
__b__ expelled	b.	forced out
__e__ plagiarism	c.	the act of providing false information
__a__ cheating	d.	to expose to danger
__c__ falsification	e.	using another's words or ideas without giving proper reference
__h__ violation	f.	unwilling

_i_ cooperative

_g_ competitive

___ calculated

_f_ reluctant

g. related to or characterized by rivalry

h. the breaking or infringement of a rule or law

i. characterized by a desire to work together

C. Words in Sentences

Read the definition of the following words and note their part of speech. Then use each one in a sentence.

1. norms [A]: ways of behavior typical of a certain group (noun)

   The norms in the school were broken by a student.

2. humbly [A]: with deference; submissively (adverb)

   His humbly was amazed by the rest of the group

3. contradict [A]: be opposed to; go against (verb)

   He always contradict his teachers

4. conducive [J]: helpful; useful (adjective)

   It's really conducive the way that the professor teachs.

5. incompetent [E]: unprofessional; not able to perform expected tasks or functions (adjective)

   It's very incompetent when a teacher humiliates to a student

6. managerial [F]: organizational (adjective)

   In must countries the teacher has a managerial role

7. administrator [P]: one who coordinates a program (noun)

   The administrator is saying his speech.

8. intimidated [T]: frightened; discouraged (verb)

   Some students intimidated each others

9. extracurricular [V]: outside of schoolwork and studies (adjective)

   In must universities there are a lots of extracurricular activities

10. participation [D]: involvement; the act of taking part (noun)

    The participation of the students is essential

11. fabrication [N]: reporting false or inaccurate information (noun)

The fabrication of false information is an example of academic dishonesty

D. Synonyms

Choose the appropriate synonym from the list to replace the italicized word, and rewrite each sentence. *Change tense, singular and plural usage, and part of speech when necessary.*

prohibited	keep
varied	official; administrative
plan	guessed
abstract	sources of assistance
emphasize	prevented from attending

1. Students find it difficult to *maintain* good grades every semester.   [K]

Students find it difficult to keep good grades every semester.

2. American institutions of higher education are sometimes criticized for being too *theoretical* and not practical.   [H]

American institutions of higer education are sometimes criticized for being too abstract and not practical

3. Give yourself time to *design* a creative project.   [H]

Give yourself time to plan a creative project

4. If you are familiar with your *resources*, you may feel more confident when problems arise.   [W]

If you are familiar with your sources of assistance, you may feel more confident when problems arise.

5. Academic success cannot always be *predicted*: many variables affect one's success.   [V]

Academic success cannot always be guessed: many variables affect one's success

6. In many high schools in the United States, it is *forbidden* to chew gum.   [A]

In many high schools in the U.S. it is prohibited to chew gum.

7. Professors of graduate classes often *stress* the importance of active participation in discussions.   [H]

Professors of graduate classes often emphasize the importance of active participation in discussions.

8. There is not always time to pursue one's *diverse* interests when studying takes up so much time.   [A]

   There is not always time to pursue one's varied interests when studying takes up so much time

9. Sometimes, students must accept *bureaucratic* details as part of their academic life.   [P]

   Sometimes, students must accept administrative details as part of their academic life

10. Students who are caught violating the honor system can be *suspended* for a certain length of time.   [M]

    Students who are caught violating the honor system can be prevented from attending for a certain length of time

E. Fill-In

First review the way the following words are used in Paragraphs J and K. Then fill in each of the blanks in the paragraph below with the word that best fits the sentence. *Note: Change the part of speech when necessary.*

innovation   [J]   deadline   [K]
subordinate   [J]   treat   [K]
egalitarianism   [J]

The School Director

The director of the private college worked very hard at his administrative duties. Each year, when applying for financial aid, he had to meet many _deadlines_. Since he had already used up private sources of funding, he needed to think of other _innovate_ ways to raise money.

Sometimes his position of authority left him isolated from his staff and students. Although he wanted an _egalitarian_ relationship with his faculty, he realized that they were his _subordinate_. He tried to _treat_ students with respect, even when he disciplined them for poor behavior.

F. Phrases and Expressions

Which statement *best* conveys the meaning of the *italicized* words?

1. If a group of people is *cliquish*, they: [V]
   a. tend to exclude nonmembers.
   b. are musical.
   c. like to have many members.

2. *Peer counseling* involves cooperation between: [U]
   a. teachers and students.
   b. students and students.
   c. teachers and parents.

3. If a teacher wants to know whether you have any *hands-on* experience in the science laboratory, she wants to know: [H]
   a. if you have any practical, applied experience.
   b. if you know the current theories.
   c. if you are right- or left-handed.

4. To *learn the ropes*, you must try to: [W]
   a. discover rules and expectations.
   b. practice sailing a boat.
   c. get tied up in an appointment.

Conversational Activities

A. Role-Playing: Teacher-Student Relationships

In pairs or in small groups, discuss what the student and/or teacher should do in the following situations. Then act out or write a dialogue about one of the situations. Make sure that you have a clear solution to each problem.

1. A student and a teacher are close friends outside the class. They have coffee together often, and even go out to movies and restaurants. Nevertheless, the student receives a *D* as the final grade for the course. The student feels that the teacher should change the grade to a *C* or a *B*.

2. In front of the class, the teacher makes an obviously incorrect statement that confuses all but one of the students. This student

knows why the teacher made the mistake and feels that it would be a good idea to clarify the misunderstanding for the rest of the class.

3. A teacher is correcting examinations and notices that three students all have the same wrong answers for every question. It is obvious that these students cheated. The teacher must do something about this.

4. A student has paid a lot of money for his courses. In one of the courses, the teacher is not doing an adequate job. The student feels that the teacher never prepares for classes, wastes time with attendance and unimportant announcements, gives poor lectures, and returns homework late. The student feels that it is necessary to say or do something.

5. In a course on world religions, one student is constantly trying to prove that her religion is the best. This student's attitude bothers the other students, and they complain to the teacher. The teacher must respond to this situation.

Discuss

1. Should teachers try to establish personal relationships with their students? Why or why not?

2. Should the teacher always be an authority figure, or should the teacher try to establish egalitarian relationships with students?

3. Should teachers be strict or lenient with students?

4. Should a student be free to express an opinion that differs from the teacher's?

B. Classroom Seating Arrangements

The following drawings illustrate the varieties of seating arrangements in the American classroom. The seating of students varies with the type of course, the number of students, and the instructor's teaching style.

Look at the differences between the seating arrangements in each classroom, and answer the questions that follow (you may choose more than one answer for each). Compare and discuss your answers with those of the other class members.

Discuss

1. Which classroom arrangement is the most formal?

2. Which is the least formal?

Seating Arrangement in Classroom

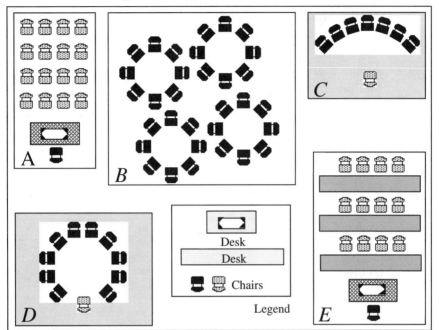

3. Which encourages the most student participation?
4. Which encourages the least student participation?
5. Which enables students to have the most eye contact with the teacher?
6. Which is preferable for language learning?
7. Which is the most common in your country?

Follow-up: A foreign student commented that she felt most comfortable in a classroom similar to that in illustration (A). She said that she felt shy and "exposed" when students had to sit in a circle or semicircle formation. Why do you think she felt this way? In which types of classroom do you feel most comfortable?

C. Common Causes of Academic Difficulty

The following list of academic problems was compiled by an international student adviser at a state university,[1] based on interviews with foreign students. For each item, first answer the question, "Is this also a problem for American students?" If you respond "yes," answer the second question, "Is this problem more serious for foreign students?" Then discuss the questions after the exercise.

Problem	Is this also a problem for American students?	Is this problem more serious for foreign students?
Student doesn't understand the system (add/drop, incompletes, testing, etc.).		
Student takes too many classes.		
Student doesn't have a good background in the subject.		
Student has English deficiency despite an adequate score on his or her English exam.		
Student is experiencing adaptation problems in the new culture and is homesick.		
Student has roommate and housing difficulties.		
Student is lonely.		
Student does not know how to study.		
Student is nervous about taking tests.		
Student cheats or plagiarizes.		

Discuss

1. Why do students have these kinds of difficulties?
2. Which problems, if any, can be prevented?

D. Seeking Information and Services in the University

Decide if the following statements are true or false, and circle either the *T* or *F*. *If the statement is false, write the correct answer in the space provided.*

1. When students have questions about their visas, they should go to the foreign student adviser.

   T   F   _____

   _____

2. When students have questions regarding electives and required courses, they should ask any professor in the department.

   T   F   _____

   _____

3. When students need letters of recommendation, they must ask the secretary of their departments to write the letters.

   T   F   _____

   _____

4. When students want to add or drop a course at the beginning of a semester, they must first go to their academic adviser for permission.

   T   F   _____

   _____

5. When students need to order transcripts to send to other universities, they must go to the department chairperson.

   T   F   _____

   _____

6. Usually, letters of recommendation and transcripts are first given directly to the student, who then sends them to another university.

   T   F   _____

   _____

7. Student health insurance enables students to get free medical care outside of school.

   T   F   _____

   _____

Discuss

1. Are these activities and services common on university campuses in your country?

2. What other activities or services exist in universities in your country?

E. Choosing University or College Courses

Study the following entries from a college course catalogue, and answer the questions that follow.[3]

Engineering
LOWER DIVISION COURSES

100. Introduction to the Engineering Profession   (2) I, II Cr/NC
Prerequisite: Not available for credit to engineering majors with 15 or more units in engineering courses.
An overall view of engineering education and professional practice. An introduction to basic skills useful in acquiring engineering problem-solving capabilities.

120. Engineering Problem Analysis   (2) I, II
One lecture and three hours of laboratory.
Prerequisite: Concurrent registration in Mathematics 150.
Analysis of engineering problems and solutions using the digital computer. Fundamentals of programming and programming language commands.

140. Engineering Measurement Analysis   (2) I, II
Prerequisite: Mathematics 140.
Methods of data presentation. Analysis and treatment of engineering data. Design of engineering experiments. Correlation and regression analysis. Practical applications are stressed.

150. Control of the Human Environment   (3)
Man's interaction with the land, water and air environment; environmental pollution; role of engineering in controlling man's environment.

299. Experimental Topics   (1–4)
Selected topics. May be repeated with new content. See Class Schedule for specific content. Limit of nine units applicable to a bachelor's degree in courses under this number, of which no more than three units may be applicable to general education requirements.

---

1. Can any engineering student take Engineering 100?
2. What does the *Cr/NC* mean in Engineering 100?
3. Does Engineering 120 have a laboratory?
4. What is the prerequisite for Engineering 140?
5. Is Engineering 140 practical or theoretical?
6. How many units does a student receive for Engineering 150?

Study the following entries from a college class schedule, and answer the questions that follow.[4]

	SERIAL NO.	COURSE NO.	SECTION NO.	COURSE TITLE	UNITS	DAYS	HOURS		BLDG. ROOM	INSTRUCTOR
■	2385	120	01	Engr Prob Analysis	2	M	1300	1350	BA 119	
		120	01	Laboratory		M	1400	1640	BA 119	
■	2387	120	02	Engr. Prob. Analysis	2	M	1300	1350	E 111	Hill J
		120	02	Laboratory		M	1400	1640	E 111	Hill J
■	2389	120	03	Engr. Prob. Analysis	2	T	800	850	E 106	Hussain E
		120	03	Laboratory		T	900	1140	E 106	Hussain E
■	2391	120	04	Engr. Prob. Analysis	2	T	1300	1350	BA 119	Chang H
		120	04	Laboratory		T	1400	1640	BA 119	Chang H
■	2393	120	05	Engr. Prob. Analysis	2	W	1300	1350	BA 119	Krishnamo
		120	05	Laboratory		W	1400	1640	BA 119	Krishnamo
■	2395	120	06	Engr. Prob. Analysis	2	Th	800	850	E 106	
		120	06	Laboratory		Th	900	1140	E 106	
■	2397	120	07	Engr. Prob. Analysis	2	Th	1300	1350	BA 119	Stone S
		120	07	Laboratory		Th	1400	1640	BA 119	Stone S
■	2399	120	08	Engr. Prob. Analysis	2	F	1300	1350	BA 119	
		120	08	Laboratory		F	1400	1640	BA 119	
■	2401	140	01	Engr. Meas. Analysis	2	MW	800	850	HH 221	Stratton F
	2402	140	02	Engr. Meas. Analysis	2	MW	900	950	HH 221	Stratton F
■	2403	140	03	Engr. Meas. Analysis	2	TTh	800	850	BA 439	
	2404	140	04	Engr. Meas. Analysis	2	TTh	900	950	SE 326	Banks J
■	2405	140	05	Engr. Meas. Analysis	2	TTh	1000	1050	SE 326	Banks J
	2406	140	06	Engr. Meas. Analysis	2	TTh	1100	1150	SE 403	
Z	2407	150	01	Control Human Env	3	TTh	930	1045	SE 121	Johnson P
■	2408	310	01	Method Of Analysis	3	TTh	1100	1215	SE 328	
■	2409	310	02	Method Of Analysis	3	MWF	1200	1250	SE 404	
■	2410	310	03	Method Of Analysis	3	TTh	1900	2015	SE 328	
■	2411	310	04	Method Of Analysis	3	MW	1730	1845	BA 121	
■	2412	310	05	Method Of Analysis	3	MW	1900	2015	SE 404	
■	2413	430	01	Princ Engr Economy	3	MWF	800	850	SE 201	Johnson P
■	2414	430	02	Princ Engr Economy	3	MWF	900	950	SE 201	Johnson P
■	2415	430	03	Princ Engr Economy	3	MW	1715	1830	SE 201	Fitz R

ENGINEERING

1. How many sections of Engineering 120 are there?
2. Who is the instructor for Engineering 120, Section 03?
3. At what time does Engineering 120, Section 04, meet? What day(s) of the week does it meet?
4. Where does Engineering 140, Section 02, meet?
5. How many times a week does Engineering 310, Section 03, meet?

F. Cross-Cultural Questions

Discuss the following questions about your own culture. Compare and contrast your responses with those of the other students.

1. Are subjects such as politics, foreign policy, and social problems taught in high school or university courses? In your opinion, should they be taught?

2. Are subjects such as marriage, sex, birth control, parenthood, and divorce taught in high school or university courses? In your opinion, should they be taught?

3. Are there any courses or subjects taught that you feel are completely useless? Are there any that should be added to the curriculum?

4. When students leave high school, are they well prepared for life outside school? Explain.

5. Does everyone receive an education? Until what age is education mandatory? Is education free?

6. Is there a separation between religion and education, or is religion part of the school curriculum?

Cultural Notes

1. During the first two years of an undergraduate education in the United States, a student must take some required courses, which are usually not part of the major. An undergraduate in engineering, for example, is required to take general courses in history, sociology, and other fields. Undergraduates generally begin to specialize in the third year, although they may have taken prerequisite courses in their major during the first two years. Students are required to take general education courses so that they become "well-rounded." Students are expected to graduate with knowledge other than that in their area of specialization.

2. The grade-point average, or GPA, is usually based on a numerical system in which *A* (excellent) = 4 points; *B* (good) = 3 points; *C* (average) = 2 points; *D* (poor) = 1 point; and *F* (fail) = no points. Students begin to accumulate their GPA during their first semester or quarter. If students let their GPA drop in the first few semesters of college, it is difficult to pick it up and maintain a high average. It is important to keep a high GPA in order to be accepted to graduate schools; some employers also want to know a student's GPA.

3. Professors decide on their own method of grading. Some instructors use the "curve" grading system, which is based on a formula that calculates a certain number of *A*s, *B*s, *C*s, *D*s, and *F*s. In other words, a professor knows what percentage of the students will

receive each grade. A student's score is calculated relative to those of the other students.

4. Academic counselors are available to help students choose classes and majors, and to arrange schedules.

5. International student advisers can help with specific problems concerning immigration, visas, and other such issues.

6. A student having difficulty with course content may see a professor during his or her office hours, which are usually posted on the office door. Professors have to limit their time with students because they have nonteaching responsibilities such as administrative work and publishing. If professors want to have a permanent position, they are obliged to publish a certain number of articles or even books. For this reason, students having difficulty at times must try to find alternative ways of seeking help.

7. Early in each quarter or semester, students sometimes take the initiative to form "study groups" in which informal learning and peer teaching takes place. It is best if this happens in the first or second week of class, as students can become lost quickly in a challenging course. Occasionally, if asked, professors and instructors may assist students in forming study groups. Generally, however, it is up to the students to do this.

8. Common Abbreviations

The following are common abbreviations related to the university:

A.A./A.S.	associate of arts/associate of science (given by a two-year college)
B.A/B.S.	bachelor of arts/bachelor of science
GPA	grade-point average
M.A./M.S.	master of arts/master of science
Ph.D.	doctorate
Prof.	professor

Subjects

econ.	economics
phys. ed. (P.E.)	physical education
math	mathematics
chem.	chemistry
bio.	biology
poli. sci.	political science
psych.	psychology
soc.	sociology

Supplementary Vocabulary and Phrases

instructor

professor

faculty

department

dean

chairperson, chairman, chairwoman

undergraduate ("undergrad")

graduate ("grad")

freshman

sophomore

junior

senior

lower division

upper division

major

minor

credits/units

credit/no credit

pass/fail

requirements

prerequisites

electives

transcript

registration

tuition

semester

quarter

to add a class

to drop a class

on-campus

off-campus

extracurricular activity

8

Work: Practices and Attitudes

"Opportunity rarely knocks on your door. Knock rather on opportunity's door if you wish to enter."

> B. C. Forbes, Founder of Forbes Magazine
> (Leading Business Magazine)

Pre-Reading Discussion

1. What do you think the above quote has to do with finding a job in the United States?

2. In the United States, finding a job requires a great deal of preparation. One must prepare a resumé with a cover letter and know how to respond appropriately in an interview. What are the steps to getting a job in your country of origin? How is this similar to or different from finding a job in the United States?

3. What do you know about relationships between employers (e.g., bosses, supervisors, and managers) and their employees in the United States? What aspects of the relationship seem to be cultural? How are employee-employer relationships different in other cultures?

241

4. In the United States, there is a strong value placed on "doing" rather than on "being." Some people refer to this as an "achievement orientation." How do you think this orientation affects people's behavior? Is achievement also emphasized in your culture?

Pre-Reading Vocabulary

1. Definition

   job search: the process of looking or "hunting" for a job

   Discussion: Have you ever been on a job search? If so, how did you learn about the job? Did people you know help you find the job?

2. Definitions

   a. **employee**: someone who works for another person or a company; a worker

   b. **employer**: someone who hires other people to work for him or her

   Discussion: In your country, is interaction between employees and employers generally formal or informal? Do employees and employers call each other by their first names?

3. Definition

   to brainstorm: to think of and express many ideas or potential solutions to a problem. The ideas are not judged, but are used creatively to generate new ideas and solutions. Subordinates and their supervisors often participate freely together in "brainstorming" sessions.

   Discussion: "Brainstorming" is popular in the business world in the United States. Why might it not be popular in other parts of the world?

4. Definition

   work ethic: an outcome of a religious belief that inspired people to work hard and achieve success

   Discussion: The American work ethic is based partly on the need to achieve and to attain material success. In your opinion, what are the various motivations for working? What are the most important rewards?

Skimming: For General Information

To get the general idea of the reading that follows:

1. Read the titles and headings of the sections.
2. Read the first and last paragraphs of the reading.

From your skimming, answer the following:

1. Is it easy for a newcomer to get a job in the United States?
2. Do all Americans have the same opinion about work?

Scanning: For Specific Information

To find specific information in the reading, look for clues such as certain words and numbers. Scan the reading to find the answers to the following:

1. What is "networking"?
2. In which paragraph can you find a definition of the word?
3. What are the hours of a typical workday in the United States?

Reading Text

Work: Practices and Attitudes

Cross-Cultural Implications of the Job Search

[A]   "Knock rather on opportunity's door if you wish to enter." "Job hunting" in the United States or in an American organization outside of the United States is a challenging experience for Americans, but it is especially so for people from other countries. A personal contact,
5   such as a friend or relative, can be of help in informing someone of a job opening and possibly helping the job applicant obtain an interview. However, this kind of "connection" (i.e., friend or family member) does not usually affect hiring decisions. Sometimes, immigrants in the United States put too much hope into what they think are good
10   job connections, and they do not fully realize how much they will have to rely on themselves to find a job. One of the biggest shocks some immigrants have upon arriving in the United States is the discovery that the government, schools, and even job placement centers do not hand people jobs on °"silver platters."

Steps to Finding a Job

[B]   The search for a skilled or professional job in the United States may first require foreign visitors or new immigrants to receive some addi-

tional training if their skills are not marketable in the United States. After that, the °job search consists of a minimum of four steps: (1) preparation; (2) networking; (3) resume development; and (4) the interview.

[C]   1. *Preparation*: This involves identifying one's skills and the °range of work one is capable of doing. It includes locating all possible sources for learning about job availability (e.g., the °classified ads in newspapers, job placement agencies, and °"headhunters"). It is also beneficial to learn something about the companies, agencies, or organizations to which one is applying for work. (Information about major corporations and organizations is available in most libraries.)

[D]   2. °*Networking*: People usually find jobs on the basis of their performance at an interview, their education, and their work experience. However, first it is important to let others know that one is looking for a job; this increases the likelihood that an °employer and °potential °employee will be brought to one another's attention. To "network" is to meet people who have similar professional interests and to widen one's circle of acquaintances for the purpose of learning

about job opportunities. The more people one knows (and informs of one's job search), the more successful that search is likely to be.
10   Participating in professional organizations and even doing volunteer work can help a job seeker let his or her capabilities be known. Having the contacts, however, is only the first step, and does not guarantee getting a job.

[E]   3. *Resume Development*: In some countries, a resume is not used as an instrument for finding a job. In the United States, however, it is one of the most important ways to °"sell oneself" to a °prospective employer. A resume is a one- or two-page summary of professional
5   goals or objectives, education, previous jobs, professional skills, accomplishments, and honors. Resumes occasionally include a little information about personal interests and hobbies.

[F]   The resume is used to communicate quickly and easily with a prospective employer. It should be visually attractive and factually correct. In a resume, people should present their experience and accomplishments very positively. However, °"padding one's resume"
5   (exaggerating one's experience and accomplishments) is not °ethical. A person who greatly exaggerates or lies on a resume can later be fired, especially if the worker lacks the skills claimed. The same

holds true for the °cover letter that should accompany the resume. This letter should describe accurately and briefly a person's professional background, and also mention the position or job in which the °applicant is interested.* There are special techniques for writing resumes and cover letters; foreign-born job applicants would be well advised to consult books on the subject and to seek help from professional resume-writing services or career centers.

[G]   4. *The Interview*: The best interview is one in which there is two-way communication between the employer and the job applicant. Often there is some °"small talk" at the beginning of the interview (e.g., "Did you have trouble finding the company?"). This "small talk" is actually very important, because the applicant's answers may indicate how easily the person can converse. A job seeker who appears unfriendly or unsociable may not be offered a position, even if the person is the most qualified. Employers look for people who seem to be likeable and easy to work with as well as technically competent.

[H]   The first few minutes of the interview are very important when it comes to making a good impression. (Some say that the first thirty seconds are °crucial.) A smile and handshake are expected after the job applicant walks into the prospective employer's office. In addition, the applicant must pay attention to certain areas related to personal appearance and °hygiene. The following list is not intended to insult readers who consider the information obvious. Applicants can make good impressions if they have:

1. Neatly trimmed hair and beard
2. Clean fingernails
3. Polished shoes
4. Clean and ironed dress or suit and tie
5. Fresh breath
6. An absence of body odors (Americans use a great deal of deodorant!)
7. An absence of strong-smelling perfume, cologne, or after-shave
8. Only a modest amount of jewelry

[I]   During the interview, a supervisor or manager (and sometimes other employees) will ask the applicant questions that must be answered fully (but without excessive detail). It is important to watch the employer's face for nonverbal cues as to whether enough has been

*For a sample resume and cover letter formats, see pp. 272–274.

5   said. It may be helpful to say something like, "Have I given you enough information, or would you like me to elaborate?" Some questions an applicant may be asked, in either a one-on-one interview or a group interview, include:

1. Tell me (or us) about yourself.
2. What do you know about this company (organization, etc.)?
3. What are your strengths and weaknesses? What do you do best?
4. In which areas do you need more experience?
5. Why did you leave your last job?
6. What are your interests outside of work?
7. How does your education and work experience relate to this job?
8. What are your career plans?
9. What do you expect to be doing in five years?

[J]   Some people may have difficulty answering certain questions because of their cultural perspectives. In cultures where humility and °modesty are virtues (e.g., in several Asian cultures), the question, "What are your strengths?" could be embarrassing. In many cultures
5   (not only Asian), people are taught not to talk or boast about their individual accomplishments. Imagine how difficult it would be for someone raised with the cultural values of humility and modesty to respond to a person of a higher status with something like, "I'm really good at administration." Or, "In my last job, I was the most °produc-
10   tive employee in my department." Yet, during an interview, an employer often wants the job °candidate to talk about his or her accomplishments. In an American interview, applicants must learn to present themselves in the most positive light. This is a challenge for many people from other countries.

[K]   As mentioned, part of the preparation for an interview involves learning about the organization. The job applicant should have questions prepared for the potential employer. If the applicant has no questions about the organization, the employer may think that the
5   person is not really interested in the job. Asking an employer about the company's product, the size of the various departments, or the method of production, for example, demonstrates the job hunter's interest.

Employer-Employee Relationships

[L]   One of the first things that foreign-born individuals notice in American companies and organizations is the casual nature of the employer-employee relationship. Among employees of different status, foreigners often observe a great deal of informal interaction (including
5   chatting and joking). It is not always clear to outsiders who is in charge.

[M]   Subordinates often call their superiors by their first names. Many foreign-born professionals find it difficult to become accustomed to this practice, and some add "Miss" or "Mr." to the first name. However, this usage (e.g., "Miss Sue" or "Mr. Michael") is very
5   unfamiliar to Americans. Similarly, most American supervisors do not like to be called "Sir" or "Ma'am." It is common, for example, for Filipino employees (i.e., new immigrants) to use these as terms of respect. However, for most American managers, "Sir" and "Ma'am" convey a position of °subservience, which goes against the American
10   cultural value of egalitarianism.

[N]   Some supervisors and managers have an °open-door office policy whereby employees may enter without appointments. This is unusual for those coming from cultures in which the society empha-

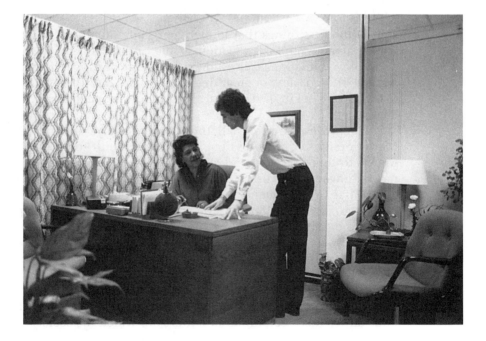

sizes rank and hierarchy. Again, the American value of egalitarianism
5 °manifests itself in casual and informal behavior among people of different status. However, even in the United States, a subordinate is not
equal to the boss. The latter has more power, earns a higher salary,
and can make decisions about hiring and firing. There is a formal
°chain of command; status and hierarchy in United States organiza-
10 tions do exist. However, outward appearances (i.e., people's interactions) do not make this fact obvious.

On-the-Job Communication Skills

[O]   What do American employers say about their foreign-born employees
with regard to communication at work? One of the first "complaints"
one hears is, "Why do some foreign employees say, 'Yes, I understand,' when in fact they do not understand? If I explain something to
5 an American and it is unclear, he or she will say, 'Wait, I didn't
understand that. Could you go over it again?'" Most American managers and co-workers do not understand some of the unspoken rules
of communication that accompany superior-subordinate relationships
in other cultures. For example, for many Chinese and Vietnamese
10 people, saying to a supervisor, "I do not understand," is considered
rude. This may indirectly imply that the supervisor did not explain
clearly, which could be insulting. However, Americans expect imme-
diate °feedback, especially when it concerns understanding an explanation, process, or procedure at work.
[P]   Similarly, people may want to know others' opinions or reactions. In meetings, co-workers (or bosses) may ask each other, "What
do you think of . . . ?" or, "What is your reaction to . . . ?" People
from some other cultures, such as the Japanese, may tend to hesitate
5 or give an answer that Americans consider to be indirect or °noncom-
mittal. They may use more silence than Americans are used to, and
say something like, "It's difficult to say," which means, "I do not
wish to respond now." Some Japanese people may feel that it is inappropriate to offer an opinion if a person of a higher status is present.
10 Additionally, the Japanese person may want to give a carefully considered answer. In contrast, many Americans like to discuss their pre-
liminary reactions and opinions even before having all the facts.
[Q]   In American business meetings, people are expected to participate verbally, or else others may think that they are uninterested in
the meeting. Active participation involves the following:

1. Initiating discussion, bringing up new ideas and topics, and making suggestions
2. Asking people for opinions, information, and explanations

3. Offering opinions and information when needed

4. Repeating ideas, information, and explanations for the rest of the group when something has not been understood

5. Summarizing information to make sure that a point has been understood

6. Encouraging people to speak by being cooperative and by accepting different points of view

If an employee appears to be passive in meetings (i.e., not participating verbally), Americans may feel that the person is not contributing to the meeting.

[R]   °"Brainstorming" is a common practice at American meetings. The purpose of brainstorming is to express as many ideas as possible on a given question or problem. This technique is used to collect all the ideas of the group, without stopping to discuss or evaluate the value of each suggestion. First people brainstorm freely; then they narrow down and °eliminate ideas or suggestions that are not °workable. Brainstorming is a creative process that demands full verbal participation. This method of creating, exploring, and solving problems is foreign to many people who are not culturally comfortable with "blurting out" ideas.

Time Considerations in the Work World

[S] °Promptness and °punctuality are major expectations in the American workplace. People who keep appointments are considered to be dependable, and those who do not are seen as unreliable. It is considered polite to call if one is going to be even a few minutes late.

5 Arriving ten minutes late to a scheduled business appointment (without having called ahead of time) is considered rude and conveys a lack of organization. Some companies have been known to fine their executives for tardiness to meetings. This American cultural concern with every minute contrasts with other cultures' views about time. In

10 many parts of Latin America, for example, arriving thirty to forty-five minutes late is not necessarily seen as disrespectful. Saying that one ran into an old friend could be a sufficient excuse for tardiness but such an explanation would not be acceptable in the American work-a-day world, where "time is money."

[T] The American workday usually begins at 8:00 A.M., 8:30 A.M., or 9 A.M., not at 8:10, 8:40, or 9:10. An employer who notices that an employee is regularly coming in several minutes late may give the employee a warning to be on time. In many countries, employees feel

5 that they can stop working if the boss is not around. Of course, this also happens in the United States but Americans (especially professionals) feel they are not using their time well if they are not productive during most of the day. Perhaps because the American culture values daily progress, there is a great emphasis on not wasting time.

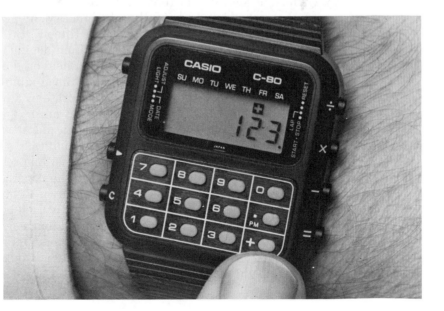

10   In the work place this value translates into a need for saving time, °budgeting time, accounting for time, and °allotting time for various activities. In business, time is carefully scheduled. Many people use appointment calendars that are printed with fifteen-, thirty-, and sixty-minute time slots. At meetings, people often decide ahead of

15   time how many minutes they will spend on each item on the agenda. Many workers have eight-to-five jobs with two fifteen-minute coffee breaks (one mid-morning and one mid-afternoon), and a forty-five minute or one-hour lunch break. These employees must °"punch the clock" every time they enter and leave their work place. Work and

20   play or work and social life are seen as distinct activities.

[U]   Some of the time-consuming °pleasantries that one sees in the business world in other countries are not part of the American business culture. For example, in an effort to "get down to business," Americans do not spend a lot of time getting to know each other well

5   before they do business. This is in contrast to Middle Eastern, Latin American, and Asian cultures where social and personal relations often must precede business relations. People from outside the United States find the pace of life in the American business world (and in people's social and personal worlds as well) to be °hectic and

10   stressful. American time has been characterized as a river flowing quickly away from people. In contrast, in other parts of the world (e.g., India), time is seen more as a pool of water that does not go anywhere. The pace of life in the American work world requires adjustment for those with a more °relaxed view of time.

Workaholics

[V]   When I started making money I just went crazy. . . . I bought a condominium and a home. I could never retire. It [work] gets inside of you. If you don't progress everyday, you feel you've wasted it. That's a day you'll never get back. . . . I usually get out of my office at one in the

5   morning. I go home and eat dinner at two. . . . I'm down at the office Saturdays too. Sundays, about half the time. The other half of the time maybe my wife and I will go horseback riding or visit a friend's house. Even when you're visiting with them, you can't get away from your work. They ask about it. It's kind of a good feeling.

Corporation President, age twenty-six[1]

[W]   Foreign-born employees often observe that Americans spend an °inordinate amount of time working and, as a consequence, have little time for leisure or personal relationships. In American English, the word °"workaholic" describes people who are as addicted to their

5   work as an alcoholic is to liquor. There are conflicting points of view about workaholics. From some points of view, they are seen as valuable members of society because they are extremely productive and °embody the values of achievement and efficiency. Increasingly, however, those concerned with problems of mental stress believe that

10   workaholics °abuse themselves physically and mentally, and that a workaholic life style is °detrimental to personal and family life. Some people are workaholics in their twenties and thirties, but in mid-life may change their priorities. Some, although certainly not all, realize that they do not have to "prove themselves" through their work

15   accomplishments and achievements.

The "Work Ethic" and Materialism

[X]   Originally, attitudes toward work in the United States were greatly influenced by the °"work ethic," which motivated people to work hard to become successful. This ethic, which originated with the Puritan colonists from England, was an °outcome of their religious

5   belief that °material success was a sign of God's favor. Work was thus °imbued with the quality of goodness. Those who achieved success were among God's "chosen" and would go to heaven.

[Y]   It would be naïve, if not incorrect, to say that today the work ethic is the main motivation for work. There is, rather, an "achievement motivation" that drives people to work hard in the United States. A strong value is placed on productiveness; people who are

5   admired in the work world are those who can produce something °tangible. This achievement orientation (or the tendency to "do" and "make") results in part from American materialism, which is an outcome of the work ethic. The harder one works, the more successful one will be. Success brings material rewards, which can be proof of

10   hard work. (This is, however, only a partial, simplistic explanation of American materialism; some materialism is based on a need for status. In addition, much of the tendency toward materialism is a result of advertising and the desire to acquire objects to enhance the quality of life.)

Reactions to Work

[Z]   No matter how employees feel about work, their primary motivation is to earn a living. People's attitudes toward their jobs are related to

the nature of their work and the rewards they receive. The twenty-six-year-old corporation president quoted above uses work to obtain
5   material goods and perhaps to avoid involvement in other aspects of his or her life. New teachers who are not tired of their jobs look for intellectual stimulation and personal gratification at work, although they are typically not highly paid. For some factory workers, work may be a °necessary evil that merely °ensures °survival.

[AA]   In the United States, one's job is an important facet of personal identity. "What do you do?" (i.e., for a living) is °synonymous with "What are you?" or "Who are you?" In American English, asking a child, "What do you want to be when you grow up?" really means,
5   "What kind of work do you want to do?" Since American society places a stronger emphasis on "doing" (including producing) than on "being," work is one of the most important activities in an individual's life. In addition, what someone "does" helps to determine that person's °prestige. A doctor has more prestige than a bus driver; an
10   accountant can claim more prestige than a waitress or a waiter.

[BB]   People are °ambivalent toward work; it is at the same time glori-
fied and °belittled. In the words of an American president,
"America's competitive spirit, the 'work ethic' of the people, is alive
and well."2 Another viewpoint is expressed in an aspirin commercial:
5 "I like my job and am good at it, but it sure °grinds me down sometimes, and the last thing I need to take home is a headache."

Comprehension Questions*

1. One of the biggest shocks that immigrants experience as newcomers to the United States is: [A]
   a. the lack of relatives who are employed.
   b. the large populations in the cities.
   c. the difficulty in finding jobs.

2. What may be required of new immigrants if their skills are not
marketable in the United States?   [B]
   additional training

*The capital letters in brackets refer to the corresponding paragraphs in the reading.

3. What are the four steps in the American job search?   [B] *preparation, networking, resume development, interview*

4. Which step of the job search emphasizes the importance of meeting people who have similar professional interests?   [C–G]

   a. learning to type

   b. creating a resume

   (c.) networking

5. Developing a resume is one of the most important ways to do what? (Use the authors' exact words.)   [E] *sell oneself to a prospective employer*

6. A resume should be: [F]

   (a.) factual.

   b. exaggerated.

   c. attractive to the eye.

   d. both (a) and (c).

   (a) NEATLY TRIMMED HAIR & BEARD
   (b) CLEAN FINGERNAILS
   (c) POLISHED SHOES
   (d) CLEAN & IRON CLOTHES
   (e) FRESH BREATH
   (f) ABSENCE OF BODY ODORS
   (g) PERFUME, COLOGNE
   (h) MODEST AMOUNT OF JEWELRY

7. The best interview is one in which: [G]

   a. the employer does all the talking.

   (b.) both the employer and the job applicant talk.

   c. the applicant does all the talking.

8. According to the authors, what are some of the ways that job applicants can make a good impression?   [H]

9. Why might it be important to watch the employer's face in an interview?   [I] *for nonverbal cues as to whether enough has been said*

10. For people from cultures that value modesty and humility, what types of questions can be difficult or embarrassing in a job interview?   [J] *What are you strengths?*

11. Asking an employer about the company demonstrates: [K]

    a. the employer's poor communication skills.

    (b.) the job applicant's interest.

    c. the job applicant's boredom.

12. In American companies, who often calls whom by their first names?   [M] *Subordinates*

    subordinates call their employers by " first name.

13. According to the authors, in what context does the American value of egalitarianism express itself in the work place?   [M, N] *to have an "open-door-policy" whereby employees may enter without appointments*

14. In what situation might an employer ask employees for their opinions?   [P] *In business meetings*

15. What is expected of people in business or work-place meetings in the United States?   [Q] *to participate verbally saying their opinions.*

16. Which of the following are examples of active participation? [Q]

  a. starting discussions and making suggestions

  b. offering and summarizing information

  c. encouraging others to speak and accepting other points of view

  (d) all of the above

17. According to the authors, brainstorming is a creative process that demands: [R]

  a. only workable ideas.

  b. thoughtful participation.

  (c.) verbal participation.

  d. both (a) and (b).

18. In the American work place, what are some consequences of tardiness and the inability to keep appointments? [S]

you may loose big projects, considered — They can take it out of your pay, fine someone

19. What do the authors suggest may be the cause of the American emphasis on not wasting time? [T]

"time is money" ← that the American culture values daily progress

20. What does the pace of life in the American work world require of people who have a less stressful concept of time? [U]

  adjustment → *speed*

21. The authors state that workaholics: [W]

  a. abuse themselves physically and mentally.

  b. are highly productive members of society.

  (c.) both (a) and (b).

22. The "work ethic" motivated people to work hard in order to become: [X]

  a. religious.

  b. Puritan.

  (c.) successful.

23. What is the primary motivation for working in the United States? What are some other motivations for working? [Z]

  to earn a living... intellectual stimulation, personal gratification

24. In the United States, the question, "What do you do?" *necessar* means [AA]

  a. What are you doing now?

  (b.) What do you do for a living?

  c. What do you do after work?

Discussion Questions

Students should prepare these before class discussion.

1. The main theme of the reading is:
    a. work values, attitudes, and practices.
    b. employer-employee relationships.
    c. materialism and competition in the work world.

2. Why is job hunting in the United States especially difficult for people from other countries?   [A]

3. In Paragraph B, the authors suggest that there are a minimum of four steps in a job search. Can you think of any other steps?

4. The authors mention several sources for learning about job availability in Paragraph C. How do people in your country find out about a job opening? Is it important to learn about the company or organization when applying for a job in your country?

5. In Paragraph E, the authors use the phrase "selling oneself." In what way do Americans have to sell or promote themselves when looking for a job? What is your reaction to this concept of "selling oneself"?

6. In Paragraph G, the authors say, "The best interview is one in which there is two-way communication between the employer and the job applicant." What is "two-way" communication?

7. In Paragraph H, the authors note that some people think that the first thirty seconds of an interview are the most important. Why do you think they believe this?

8. According to the authors in Paragraph J, why would a question like, "Tell me about yourself," be difficult for some people? From your cultural point of view, is it acceptable to discuss one's accomplishments?

9. In Paragraphs L, M, and N, the authors say that the informality of American employer-employee interaction is difficult for some foreigners and new immigrants to understand. Are the interactions between employers and employees in your country similar to or different from those of the Americans?

10. In Paragraphs Q–R, the authors describe the active participation that is expected of employees in an American business meeting. Is this similar to expectations of employees in your country? Are feedback and the open discussion of ideas and opinions acceptable in the business world in your country?

11. If, as the authors say in Paragraph U, American time can be viewed as a river flowing quickly away, then people will tend to "race with the clock" or attempt to "beat time." How would a different view of time affect behavior? Give examples.

12. Reread the quote in Paragraph V. How many days per week do people in your country work? How much time do they spend on leisure activities? Do they spend their free time with their families?

13. In Paragraph W, the term "workaholic" is described. Do you know anybody like this? Is "workaholism" a phenomenon in your culture?

14. According to the authors' discussion in Paragraph W, why do Americans have conflicting views about "workaholics"? How do you feel about "workaholism"?

15. The "work ethic" that the authors describe in Paragraph X was based on the concept of delayed reward (people enjoyed their success only after they got to heaven). Do you think this concept still motivates most Americans to work hard? Based on what you know about American society, do you think a work ethic exists today? Is there a work ethic in your country of origin?

16. In Paragraph Y, the authors offer a partial and simplistic explanation of American materialism as it relates to the work ethic. What else accounts for American materialism?

17. In Paragraph Z, the authors mention that the twenty-six-year-old corporation president may use work as a way of avoiding involvement in other aspects of his life. What could the authors be referring to? What priorities do many people in your country agree upon, such as spending time with the family, pursuing interests, enjoying leisure time, playing sports, and working?

18. The authors say in Paragraph AA that many Americans consider "doing" to be more important than "being." In your culture, which do you think is more highly valued? Give an example that shows why.

19. There is a saying in English, "The devil makes work for idle hands." Can you explain this expression? Can you think of any sayings from your native language that reflect your culture's emphasis on either "doing" or "being"? Explain the saying.

20. A sociologist named Emile Durkheim noted that in some societies, people's basic identity comes from their jobs and not from any other aspect of themselves. Do you think that Americans

define themselves in terms of their jobs? In your culture, what gives people their identities? How important is work compared to other activities in life?

Vocabulary Exercises

Vocabulary List

As you read the vocabulary list below, find two or three words you already know. Give their definitions.

Paragraph C
range - *clasificar*

Paragraph D
networking
employer - *jefe, dueño*
potential
employee - *empleado*

Paragraph E
resume
prospective

Paragraph F
ethical - *moral*
applicant - *candidato*

Paragraph H
crucial
hygiene

Paragraph J
modesty
productive
candidate

Paragraph M
subservience
subordinación

Paragraph N
manifests

Paragraph O
feedback - *retroalimentación*
regeneración

Paragraph P
noncommittal
reservado
indeciso

Paragraph R
brainstorming
eliminate
workable

Paragraph S
promptness *prontitud*
punctuality

Paragraph T
budgeting *presupuesto*
allotting *distribuir*

Paragraph U
pleasantries
hectic
relaxed

Paragraph W
inordinate *excesivo*
embody - *personificar*
abuse
detrimental - *perjudicial*
nocivo

Paragraph X
outcome *resultado*
consecuencia
materia
imbued *manipular*
meterle ideas
en la cabeza

Paragraph Y
tangible - *conveniente*

Paragraph Z
evil - *perverso*
ensures *asegurar*
survival - *supervivencia*

Paragraph AA	*Paragraph BB*
synonymous	ambivalent mixed feelings (confuse)
prestige	belittled – disminuir
	grinds – oprimir, triturar

Phrases and Expressions

esfuerzo

silver platter [A]: something that has come with no effort. Example: The job was handed to him on a silver platter

job search [B]: the process of looking for a job

classified ads [C]: section in newspaper which lists jobs available

headhunters [C]: people who help place job applicants in jobs and are paid for it

selling oneself [E]: convincing another person, as in an interview, why you are the best person for the job

padding one's resume [F]: exaggerating one's accomplishments in a resume

cover letter [F]: letter explaining who you are and what type of work you are looking for

small talk [G]: superficial talk on subjects that are not serious

open-door office policy [N]: policy whereby employees may enter their bosses' offices at any time

chain of command [N]: hierarchy; example: president, vice president, manager, etc.

punch the clock [T]: signing in when coming to work and leaving work

workaholic [W]: someone who is "addicted" to work

work ethic [X]: a philosophy which drives people to work hard and make work central in their lives

necessary evil [Z]: something that has to be done

A. Matching

Match the words with their definitions. Place the letter of the definition in the space next to the word.

belittlement (n)
make someone less

_g_ evil (adj/n)   a. critical response; reaction

_h_ outcome   b. relieved from stress

_k_ ambivalent (adj)   c. made to seem little or less important

_c_ belittled   d. distributing; assigning

_j_ grinds   e. the act of looking for employment

f. thinking of; expressing

grind
ground } salt, pepper, coffee
grind

relaxation (n)

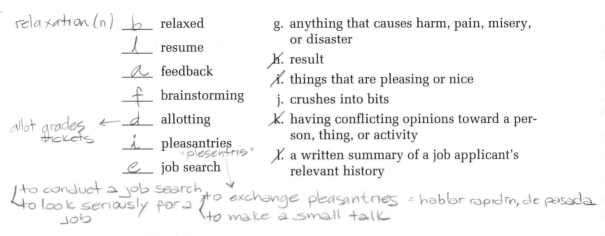

_b_ relaxed

_l_ resume

_a_ feedback

_f_ brainstorming

allot grades ← _d_ allotting
tickets

_i_ pleasantries
"plesentris"

_e_ job search

g. anything that causes harm, pain, misery, or disaster

h. result

i. things that are pleasing or nice

j. crushes into bits

k. having conflicting opinions toward a person, thing, or activity

l. a written summary of a job applicant's relevant history

to conduct a job search,
to look seriously for a { to exchange pleasantries = hablar rapidm, de pasada
job { to make a small talk

B. Word Forms

Decide which part of speech is needed in the blanks in the sentences below. Change the original word to the appropriate form.

1. applicant [F]

a. Today, my friend is _applying_ for a new job at the factory.

b. There are many _applicants_ for the job, so the competition is great.

c. Yesterday, five other people _applied_ for the job.

2. detrimental [W]

a. Smoking has been found to be _detrimental_ to a person's health.

b. A lack of exercise is also a _detriment_ to good health.

3. employee, employer [D]

a. I am an _employee_ of the Coca-Cola Company; I work seven hours every day at the factory.

b. The owner of the grocery store has _employed_ many good people for years.

c. Sometimes, _employers_ are generous about the amount of time their workers can take off for vacation.

d. People who are unhappy with their jobs should seek _employment_ elsewhere.

4. productive   [J]

    a. The quality of work a person _produces_ depends on the amount of time and thought that she puts into her efforts.

    b. I am most _productive_ if I have had a good night's sleep and a healthy breakfast.

    c. Some employees are evaluated in terms of their _productivity_

5. synonymous   [AA]

"sinonim"   a. A _synonym_ "deciv" of the verb "to deceive" is "to trick."

    b. The question "What do you do?" is _synonymous_ with "What job do you have?"

6. survival   [Z]

    a. When the airplane crashed, there were few _survivors_ .

    b. _to survival_ in the desert requires an adequate water supply.

    c. Plants cannot _survive_ if they do not receive sunlight.

7. prestige   [AA]

    a. Is Harvard University more _prestigious_ than Yale?

    b. Some people think that _prestige_ is not important.

8. ethical   [F]

    a. The firing of the employees was not an _ethical_ thing to do.

    b. The "work _ethic_" has its influence on people today.

    c. The lawyer's _ethics_ were questioned when he charged his clients too much money.

9. material   [X]

    a. One kind of _material_ that is used to build houses is wood. (singular) (singular)

    b. Some people try very hard to gain _material_ wealth.

    c. _materialism_ is the concept that places the highest value on having things.

    d. _materialistic_ societies have little in common with spiritualistic ones.

"espirtualistic" = spiritualistic
"materialistic" = materialistic

C. Words in Sentences

Read the definition of the following words and note their part of speech. Then use each one in a sentence.

1. range [C]: type; extent (noun)

    Here is the list of the employments' range

2. prospective [E]: possible; expected (adjective)

    There are a lot of prospective projects

✗ 3. hygiene [H]: cleanliness (noun)

    He knows an excellent manners of hygiene

✗ 4. workable [R]: practical; feasible (adjective)

    He's always workable in his office

5. abuse [W]: mistreatment (noun)

    The boss abuses of his employees

✗ 6. tangible [Y]: real; not abstract (adjective)

    He works in a very tangible Company

✗ 7. ensures [Z]: guarantees (verb)

    This product has a good ensures

D. Synonyms

Choose the appropriate synonym from the list to replace the italicized word, and rewrite each sentence. *Change tense, singular and plural usage, and part of speech when necessary.*

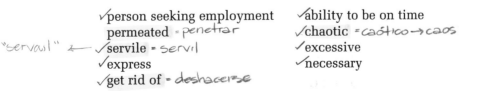

✓person seeking employment   ✓ability to be on time
  permeated = penetrar   ✓chaotic = castico → caos
"servail" ←— ✓servile = servil   ✓excessive
  ✓express   ✓necessary
  ✓get rid of = deshacerse

1. The *candidate* for the job was very well qualified.   [J]

    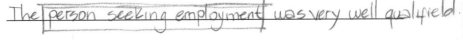

    The person seeking employment was very well qualifield.

2. Your attendance at the meeting is *crucial* to the success of the project.   [H]

Your attendance at the meeting is [necessary] to the success of the proyect.

3. To *eliminate* the problem, a solution must be found.   [R]

To [get rid of] the problem, a solution must be found

4. American values *manifest* themselves in daily life.   [N]

American values [express] themselves in daily life

5. Her *promptness* in accomplishing the task helped her get an increase in salary.   [S]

Her [ability to be on time] in accomplishing the task helped her get an increase in salary

6. Some Americans spend an *inordinate* amount of time working.   [W]

Some Americans spend an [excessive] amount of time working

7. Many Americans are not comfortable with jobs that require *subservient* relationships with employees.   [M]

Many Americans aren't comfortable with jobs that require [servil] relationships with employees

8. Today was *hectic* because I did not organize my goals.   [U]

"keiotic"   *Today was [chaotic] 'cause I didn't organize my goals*

9. The "work ethic" *imbued* work with the quality of goodness.   [X]

"permieited"   *The "work ethic" [permeated] work with the quality of goodness.*

E. Definitions in Context

Try to guess the meaning of the *italicized* word by looking at its context in the sentence. Write a definition in the space provided. Check your dictionary only after you have tried to determine the meaning yourself.

1. The *potential* employee was well qualified but was not hired until a month after the interview.   [D]

possible, expected. / future

2. My friend figured out a plan for *networking* to help her find a job as a teacher: she would attend the next national conference of educators and meet new people.   [D]

chain of interconnected people, arrangment. /

3. The employer made her preference for *modesty* in dress clear; she told her employees not to wear short sleeves, short skirts, or short pants.   [J]

   moderate, showy in appearance. /

4. Because the speaker did not seem to have a distinct opinion about the world economy, people thought he was *noncommittal*.   [P]

   ~~confused~~, not showing what one thinks. / not expressing her opinion or intention

5. I bought a calendar with time slots, and now I can start *budgeting* my time more effectively.   [T]

   plan of income, do not waste time. / separate into parts

6. Hard-working employees *embody* the values of efficiency and achievement.   [W]

   express ideas in a visible form. / symbolize

F. Phrases and Expressions

Which statement *best* conveys the meaning of the *italicized* words?

1. When someone expects a job to be handed to her on a *silver platter*, she means that: [A]

   a. tonight's dinner will be delicious.

   (b) she expects a job to be offered to her.

   c. she expects to work hard to find a job.

2. An employer with an *open-door office policy:*   [N]

   (a) expects people to come to her freely with questions and concerns.

   b. is concerned about upper management.

   c. has a broken door that she cannot control.

3. A *workaholic:*   [W]

   a. works so much that he does not have time to pursue other interests.

   b. is as addicted to work as an alcoholic is addicted to alcohol.

   (c) both (a) and (b).

4. To people who regard work as a *necessary evil:*   [Z]

   a. work is the result of the devil.

   b. work must be evil; there is no choice.

   (c) work is necessary, but undesirable.

5. Many workers dislike having to *punch the clock:*
a. fight with time.
b. sign in when they come to work and when they leave.
c. remove the clock.

Conversational Activities

[handwritten: Read it and a paragraph]

A. Quotations on Work

Following are religious, literary, and comical quotations on the subject of work. Read them and discuss the questions that follow.

Quotations

[handwritten: Due Thursday / 1 paragraph]

You shall gain your bread by the sweat of your brow.

[handwritten: You work hard]

Genesis 3:19

[handwritten: Which one expresses Mr. Morita attitude work... (why?)]

Hire yourself out to work which is beneath you rather than become dependent on others.   *[handwritten: be independent]*

[handwritten: You should support yourself, independent person] Talmud (religious writings)

*[handwritten: * Intro]*

You work that you may keep peace with the earth and the soul of the earth. *[handwritten: working for others / work together]*

*[handwritten: * Body, examples.]*

[handwritten: It might be cooperative, to have peace]

Kahlil Gibran

*[handwritten: * Conclu]*

Work and love—these are the basics. Without them there is neurosis. *[handwritten: phychological mental problem]*

[handwritten: a balance of them]   *[handwritten: BALANCE]*   Theodor Reik, *Of Love and Lust*

[handwritten: imbalance]

"Nothing is really work unless you would rather be doing something else." *[handwritten: ENJOY WORK]*

[handwritten: When we work we should be doing something that we really enjoy it]

Sir James Barrie, as quoted in *Reader's Digest*, October 1936

"You can't eat for eight hours a day nor drink for eight hours a day nor make love for eight hours a day—all you can do for eight hours is work. Which is the reason why man makes himself and everybody else so miserable and unhappy."

[handwritten: He dislike work]

[handwritten: He has to work 8 hrs. a day]   William Faulkner

[handwritten: He like to eat, drink, eat, make love but]

Discuss

[handwritten: WORK UNNECESSARY EVIL]

1. What does each of these quotations say about the nature of work?

2. Do they reflect your feelings about work?

3. Do you know any quotes or expressions about work in your language?

B. Resumes

If you are going to look for a job in the United States, there are some specific "Do's" and "Don'ts" to keep in mind when you are writing your resume:[3]

Do	*Don't*
Make sure that your resume has been proofread by someone else.	Exaggerate or lie about your experiences.
Have your resume printed professionally.	Underestimate the importance of your experiences.
Write succinctly.	Include information about salary.
Limit your resume to one page, if possible.	Use personal pronouns or abbreviations.
Make your resume visually attractive.	Explain why you left your previous jobs.
Use good-quality white, off-white, or gray paper.	Put personal information (e.g., height, weight, or marital status).

Sample formats[4] for two types of resumes—a chronological resume and a skill resume—appear on pp. 272 and 273. After you have studied each, prepare drafts of both types of resumes.

C. Cover Letters

The cover letter that one submits with a resume can be as important as the resume itself. Read the explanation[5] of what to include in a cover letter on p. 274 and then write your own letter.

D. Job Prestige

In 1961, the sociologist Otis Duncan devised a scale that indicated how much prestige particular jobs or occupations in the United States carried.[6] (For the Duncan Scale, see p. 280.)

Directions: Individually, rank the following fourteen occupations in terms of the status they carry in your country; record your responses on the chart on p. 275. (This ranking is not necessarily what *you* think, but rather indicates your country's views of the occupations.)

(Text continues on p. 275)

Chronological Resume

Name
Address (city, state, zip code)
Telephone number (with area code)

JOB OBJECTIVE: _____

_____

EDUCATION: University   Location
Degree, date of graduation, major, GPA, significant
courses, honors, school projects

High School   Location
Date of graduation, class rank or GPA, honors

EXPERIENCE: Organization   Location
Job title, duties and accomplishments, projects
  Dates
_____

_____

Organization   Location
Job title, duties and accomplishments, projects
  Dates
_____

_____

INTERESTS: _____

_____

REFERENCES: Available upon request. (Optional)

Functional Resume

Name
Address (city, state, zip code)
Telephone number (with area code)

JOB OBJECTIVE: _____

_____

SKILLS: (Write 3–5 separate sections (as below), paragraphs, each focusing on an area of expertise or skill. Include accomplishments related to your job objective, giving examples whenever possible.)

Computer Programming (example of a skill)

• _____

_____

Financial Planning (example of a skill)

• _____

_____

Training and Development (example of a skill)

• _____

_____

WORK/ PROFESSIONAL EXPERIENCE:	Organization	Location
	Job title	Dates
	Organization	Location
	Job title	Dates

EDUCATION: University   Location
Degree, date of graduation, major, GPA, significant courses, honors

PROFESSIONAL ASSOCIATIONS: (List membership and/or participation in significant professional associations.)

REFERENCES: Available upon request. (Optional)

Sample Cover Letter

Street Address
City, State, Zip
Date

Name, Title
Company Name
Street Address
City, State, Zip

Dear _____:

Paragraph 1. *Attract attention.* State who you are, why you are writing, and how you heard of the opening or the employer. Reference should be made to your specific interest in this organization and position.

Paragraphs 2, 3. *Arouse interest.* Here you can "editorialize," and amplify your unique qualifications and accomplishments. Do not simply restate information from your resume, but rather draw conclusions, summarize, and indicate how your experiences and skills can be utilized in this organization and position.

Paragraph 4. *Indicate action.* State what action you will take (e.g., a follow-up phone call or letter) and when. The employer may wish to contact you first. Make this easy for the employer by providing current telephone numbers and area codes, and changes in address. Indicate when you will be available for an interview. State that you are enclosing a copy of your resume.

Sincerely yours,
Signature
Typed Name

Then, in small groups, compare your rankings. Together, reach a consensus (agreement) as to the degree of prestige each occupation should have. This second ranking will be based on your personal opinion. After you do this, discuss the questions on p. 276.

Occupations

banker	religious leader
writer	factory owner
doctor	labor union organizer
undertaker	college professor
elementary school teacher	corporate president
assembly-line worker	nuclear physicist
farmer	carpenter

Individual Ranking	**Consensus Ranking**
According to Country	*Based on Group Opinion*
1. ————————	1. ————————
2. ————————	2. ————————
3. ————————	3. ————————
4. ————————	4. ————————
5. ————————	5. ————————
6. ————————	6. ————————
7. ————————	7. ————————
8. ————————	8. ————————
9. ————————	9. ————————
10. ————————	10. ————————
11. ————————	11. ————————
12. ————————	12. ————————
13. ————————	13. ————————
14. ————————	14. ————————

Discuss

1. Was it difficult to reach a consensus on occupational prestige with your group?
2. What determines overall prestige in your country (money, education, family name, another factor)?

E. Role-Playing

Working in small groups with members of the same culture, act out one of the following situations (or choose another situation with your group). After each role-play, answer the questions that follow.

1. A boss in a factory speaks to a group of workers about the high rate of absenteeism. The workers are not happy with the new rules and regulations.
2. A lazy employee of a company receives a raise because the boss is a relative. The other employees are angry.
3. An employee is fired for no apparent reason.
4. A secretary cannot finish her work because the boss is always bothering her.
5. An eighteen-year-old high school graduate is having trouble deciding which career to follow. Her parents are discussing the problem.
6. A company vice president has been caught cheating on the financial accounts.

Discuss

1. Is the problem you selected to act out a typical one in your country?
2. Could it happen in any country?

F. Work Attitudes in the United States

In the 1970s, the author Studs Terkel spent three years interviewing workers in the United States to find out how they felt about their jobs. He compiled the interviews in *Working* which, for several weeks, became the best-selling book in the United States. Read the following excerpts from a few of his interviews. Then, in small groups, choose one or more of the passages to discuss.* As a group,

*Groups should choose different passages.

write a list of the positive and/or negative qualities that the workers attribute to their jobs. For example:

A Teacher in the United States

> Likes to help people learn
>
> Dislikes low salary
>
> Has too much work to do at night
>
> Likes the stimulation of the other teachers
>
> Is intellectually stimulated

Individually, make a list of how you think a worker in your country would feel about the same job. Compare lists.

Garbage Man

> I've been outside for seven years and I feel more free. I don't take the job home with me. When I worked in the office, my wife would say, "What was the matter with you last night? You laid there and your fingers were drumming the mattress." That's when I worked in the office. The bookkeeping and everything else, it was starting to play on my nerves. Yeah, I prefer laboring to bookkeeping. For one thing, a bookkeeping job doesn't pay anything. I was the lowest paid man there.[7]

Policeman

> I make an arrest on someone who commits a crime of violence. I have to resort to a physical type of arrest to subdue him. I might have to shoot the person. I'm chastised for being brutal. It's all right for him to do what he wants to do against myself or legitimate people, but in no way can I touch him. I don't see the justice.[8]

Dentist

> Dentistry is very precise. No matter what you do, sometimes things just don't go right. One of the big diseases dentists have is stress. It's physically hard because you're in an uncomfortable position most of the day. With techniques today, young fellows are sitting down. I wish I'd sit down more, but I'm not accustomed to it. So I stand most of my day. . . . The patients are in a tense position too. There is stress on both sides. . . . All they have to do is jerk once on you and they've damaged themselves.[9]

Waitress

> People imagine a waitress couldn't possibly think or have any kind of aspiration other than to serve food. When somebody says to me, "You're great, how come you're *just* a waitress?" *Just* a waitress. I'd say,

"Why, don't you think you deserve to be served by me?" It's implying that he's not worthy, not that I'm not worthy. It makes me irate. I don't feel lowly at all. I myself feel sure I don't want to change the job. I love it.[10]

Steel Mill Worker

[My boss] said, "Mike, you're a good worker but you have a bad attitude." My attitude is that I don't get excited about my job. I do my work but I don't say whoopee-doo. The day I get excited about my job is the day I go to a head shrinker [psychiatrist]. How are you gonna get excited about pullin' steel? How are you gonna get excited when you're tired and want to sit down?

It's not just the work. Somebody built the pyramids. Pyramids, Empire State Building—these things just don't happen. There's hard work behind it. I would like to see a building, say, the Empire State, I would like to see on one side of it a foot-wide strip from top to bottom with the name of every bricklayer, the name of every electrician, with all the names. So when a guy walked by, he could take his son and say, "See, that's me over there on the forty-fifth floor. I put the steel beam in." Picasso can point to a painting. What can I point to? A writer can point to a book. Everybody should have something to point to.[11]

Follow-up: When you compared your individual lists, what cultural differences and similarities in worker attitudes did you discover?

G. Cross-Cultural Questions

Answer the following questions about your own culture, and then discuss intercultural similarities and differences.

1. How does a person decide on a career (e.g., with the help of parents, school counselors, etc.)?
2. When do young people begin thinking about finding jobs?
3. What are typical working hours? Do people take work home? How much socializing is there on a job?
4. What obligations do employers and employees have toward each other? Do employees stay on one job for a long time or is there a great deal of job mobility?
5. What benefits do employees have (e.g., health insurance, vacation, etc.)?
6. How do people advance on the job? Is advancement based on competency or seniority?

7. What jobs are considered "male" jobs and "female" jobs? Does the sex of an employee affect one's work, status, or salary on the job?

8. What kind of economy does your country have (e.g., capitalist, socialist, etc.)? How does it affect workers and the nature of occupations?

Cultural Notes

1. "Blue-collar worker" is a term referring to manual laborers and skilled and unskilled workers. "White-collar worker" refers to such employees as salespersons, clerks, secretaries, technicians, managers, and "professionals" (lawyers, doctors, etc.).

2. A "union" is an organization of wage earners formed to protect the worker with respect to wages and working conditions.

3. "Minimum wage" refers to the lowest amount of money an employer can pay an employee over the age of eighteen. In 1970, the minimum wage was $1.30 per hour; in 1980, it was $3.10. In 1990, it was $4.25.

4. In the United States, job advancement and mobility are determined not only by employers. Employees themselves may independently decide to leave their employer because of the promise of a better job elsewhere. An employee is expected to be loyal to the employer while on the job but is free to change jobs whenever the worker wishes. Scientists, engineers, highly educated professionals, executives, technicians, and managers have particularly high rates of job mobility.

5. In the United States, the government recognizes the importance of work as the means for survival, and has established several systems of compensation for people who are unemployed or underemployed. "Social Security" is paid to disabled and retired persons. "Welfare," including food stamps, goes to poor people and unemployed immigrants. Some retired people also receive a "pension" based on the number of years they worked at one job.

6. The average amount of time Americans have for vacation is generally between two and four weeks per year. Vacation time generally increases with the time an employee has worked in one place.

7. The following is the Duncan Scale of job prestige in the United States.[12] The occupations are ranked in order of prestige, from top to bottom.

The Duncan Scale of Job Prestige

Physicians
Lawyers and judges
Architects
Aeronautical engineers
Social scientists
Natural scientists
Salaried managers in
  manufacturing
Authors
Stock and bond salespeople
Teachers, retail store buyers
Insurance agents and brokers
Actors, librarians
Retail-trade managers
Local public administrators
Manufacturing foremen
Athletes, clergymen, bank tellers
Power station operators
Sales clerks
Nurses
Construction foremen
Bill collectors, detec-
  tives, dieticians,
  furriers

Plumbers and steam
  fitters
Building managers
Plasterers
Bus drivers
Bakers
Motor vehicle manu-
  facturing operators
Automobile mechanics
Members of the armed
  forces
Blast furnace operators
Waiters and waitresses
Farmers
Taxi drivers, charwom-
  en, paperhangers,
  fishermen
Peddlers and manu-
  facturing laborers
Farm laborers
Coal miners, yarn-,
  thread-, and fabric-
  mill machinery
  operators

Supplementary Vocabulary and Phrases

occupation
advancement
income
wages
merit
raise
benefits
overtime
retirement
to apply for a job
to be qualified for a job

to earn the bread
to lay off
to fire
to quit
to resign
to exploit
"bread and butter"
blue-collar worker
white-collar worker
labor unions
manual labor

Endnotes

Preface

1. Winston Brembeck, "The Development and Teaching of a College Course in Intercultural Communication," *Readings in Intercultural Communication*, v. 2 (Pittsburgh: SIETAR Publications, University of Pittsburgh, March 1977), p. 14.

Cross-Cultural Terms and Principles

1. Sharon Ruhly, *Orientations to Intercultural Communication: Modules in Speech Communication* (Science Research Associates, Inc., 1976), p. 4.

Chapter 1

1. Adapted from Robert L. Kohls, "The Values Americans Live By" (Washington, D.C.: Meridian House International, 1984), pp. 4–15. Reprinted by permission of the author.
2. Adapted from Janet Gaston, "Cultural Orientation in the English as a Second Language Classroom," in *Beyond Experience,* ed. Donald Batchelder and Elizabeth G. Warner (Brattleboro, Vt.: The Experiment Press, 1977), pp. 95, 96. Reprinted by permission.
3. Adapted from Andrea L. Rich and Dennis H. Ogawa, "Intercultural and Interracial Communication: An Analytical Approach," in *Intercultural Communication: A Reader*, ed. Larry A. Samovar and Richard E. Porter (Belmont, Calif.: Wadsworth Publishing Co., 1976), p. 26.

4. Modified with permission from Richard E. Porter and Larry A. Samovar, "Basic Principles of Intercultural Communication," in *Intercultural Communication: A Reader*, 2nd ed., ed. Larry A. Samovar and Richard E. Porter (Belmont, Calif.: Wadsworth Publishing Co., 1991), p. 13.

5. Ibid., p. 12.

6. Developed by Jill Sofia, ESL instructor, American Language Institute, San Diego State University, 1979. Reprinted by permission.

7. Adapted from Henry Holmes and Stephen Guild, "The Parable," in *Intercultural Sourcebook: Cross-Cultural Training Methodologies*, ed. David S. Hoopes and Paul Ventura (LaGrange Park, Ill.: Intercultural Network, Inc., SIETAR, 1979), pp. 155–57. (Parable originally designed by Sidney Simon, professor of education, University of Massachusetts.) Reprinted by permission.

Chapter 2

1. Kalvero Oberg, "Culture Shock and the Problem of Adjustment," in *Toward Internationalism*, ed. Elise C. Smith and Louise Fiber Luce (Rowley, Mass.: Newbury House, 1979), p. 43.

2. Adapted by permission of the publisher from *Bring Home the World: A Management Guide for Community Leaders of International Programs*, Stephen H. Rhinesmith, pp. 55–56, ©1975 by Amacon, a division of American Management Association. All rights reserved.

3. Excerpts adapted from essays written by international students, San Diego State University, 1979.

4. Adapted by permission of the publisher from *Bring Home the World: A Management Guide for Community Leaders of International Programs*, Stephen H. Rhinesmith, pp. 55–56, ©1975 by Amacon, a division of American Management Association. All rights reserved.

5. Adapted from Robert Kohls, "Reaching Consensus," in *Intercultural Sourcebook: Cross-Cultural Training Methodologies*, ed. David S. Hoopes and Paul Ventura (LaGrange Park, Ill.: Intercultural Network, Inc., SIETAR, 1979), p. 160.

Chapter 3

1. Winston Brembeck, "The Development and Teaching of a College Course in Intercultural Communication," *Readings in Intercultural Communication*, v. 2 (Pittsburgh: SIETAR Publications, University of Pittsburgh, March 1977), p. 14.

2. Deborah Tannen, *You Just Don't Understand: Women and Men in Conversation* (New York: Ballantine Books, 1990), p. 196.

3. Ibid., p. 207.

4. Adapted from Nancy Sakamoto and Reiko Naotso, *Polite Fictions: Why Japanese and Americans Seem Rude* (Tokyo: Kinseido Ltd., 1982), p. 81.

5. Ibid., p. 83.

Chapter 4

1. Edward T. Hall, *The Silent Language* (Greenwich, Conn.: A Fawcett Premier Book, 1959), p. 39.
2. Albert Mehrabian and Morton Wiener, "Decoding of Inconsistent Communications," *Journal of Personality and Social Psychology*, 6 (1967), 109–14; Albert Mehrabian and Susan R. Ferris, "Inference of Attitudes from Nonverbal Communication in Two Channels," *Journal of Consulting Psychology*, 31 (1967), 248–52.
3. This phrase is from Hall, *The Silent Language*.
4. Edward T. Hall, *The Hidden Dimension* (Garden City, N.Y.: Doubleday & Company, 1966), pp. 126–27.
5. Peter Collett, "Training Englishmen in the Nonverbal Behavior of Arabs," *International Journal of Psychology* 6 (1971), 209–15.
6. Hall, *The Hidden Dimension*, 1966, pp. 126–27.

Chapter 5

1. U.S. Department of Commerce, Bureau of the Census, *Population Profile of the United States, 1989*, Current Population Reports, Special Studies, Series P-23, No. 159 (Washington, D.C., 1989), p. 2.
2. Adapted from John C. Condon and Fathi Yousef, *An Introduction to Intercultural Communication* (Indianapolis: Bobbs-Merrill, 1975), pp. 43, 44. Reprinted by permission.
3. Ibid., p. 44.
4. Great Expectations. 16830 Ventura Blvd., Suite P, Encino, California (818) 788–5200. Used with permission.

Chapter 6

1. U.S. Department of Commerce, Bureau of the Census, *Population Profile of the United States, 1989*, Current Population Reports, Special Studies, Series P-23, No. 159 (Washington, D.C., 1989), p. 3.
2. Eugene Richards, "The American Family," *Life*, April 1991, p. 26.
3. *Population Profile of the United States, 1989*, p. 3.
4. Ibid., pp. 40, 41.
5. Ibid., p. 28.
6. K. A. London, *Cohabitation, Marriage, Marital Disillusionment, and Remarriage: United States, 1988*, Advanced Data from Vital and Health Statistics, No. 194 (Hyattsville, Md.: National Center for Health Statistics, 1990).
7. Ibid.
8. "Disciplining Children: Parents Say Spanking OK," *Contra Costa [California] Times*, January 8, 1991, family section.
9. Adapted from Sophie Smith Hollander, *Impressions of the United States* (New York: Holt, Rinehart and Winston, 1964), pp. 145–49. Reprinted by permission.

Chapter 7

1. *Northwestern University Student Handbook,* No. 4 (Evanston, Ill.: North-western University, September 1990), p. 65.
2. Ibid., p. 61.
3. Excerpted from the San Diego State University Catalogue and Schedule, Spring Semester, 1979.
4. Ibid.

Chapter 8

1. Adapted from Studs Terkel, *Working: People Talk About What They Do All Day and How They Feel About What They Do* (New York: Pantheon Books, A Division of Random House, 1974), pp. 603–6. Reprinted by permission.
2. Excerpted from a speech given by Richard Nixon on Labor Day, 1971, and reprinted in ibid., p. xi.
3. Adapted from *Job Placement Handbook*, Northwestern University Placement Center, Evanston, Illinois, prepared by Victor Linquist, Director, 1991.
4. Ibid.
5. Ibid.
6. Peter M. Blau and Otis Dudley Duncan, *The American Occupational Structure* (New York: John Wiley & Sons, 1964), pp. 122, 123.
7. Terkel, *Working*, pp. 150–51.
8. Ibid., p. 183.
9. Ibid., p. 328.
10. Ibid., p. 391.
11. Ibid., p. 2.
12. Blau and Duncan, *The American Occupational Structure*, pp. 122, 123.

Bibliography

Books

Adelman, Mara B. Cross-Cultural Adjustment: A Theoretical Perspective on Social Support. *Intercultural Journal of International Relations.* 12:183–204, 1988.

Bellah, Robert N., et al. *Habits of the Heart: Individualism and Commitment in American Life.* New York: Harper and Row, 1985.

Brislin, Richard W. *Cross-Cultural Encounters: Face-to-Face Interaction.* New York: Pergamon Press, 1981.

Condon, John, and Fathi Yousef. *An Introduction to Intercultural Communication.* Indianapolis, Ind.: Bobbs-Merrill, 1977.

Gudykunst, W. B., and Y. Y. Kim. *Communicating with Strangers.* Reading, Mass.: Addison-Wesley, 1984.

Hall, Edwards. *The Hidden Dimension.* Garden City, N.Y.: Doubleday, 1966.

———. *Beyond Culture.* Garden City, N.Y.: Doubleday, 1966.

Levine, Deena R., Jim Baxter, and Piper McNulty. *The Culture Puzzle: Cross-Cultural Communication for English as a Second Language.* Englewood Cliffs, N.J.: Prentice Hall, 1987.

Harris, Phillip R., and Robert T. Moran. *Managing Cultural Differences: Strategies for Global Management.* Houston: Gulf, 1990.

Samovar, Larry A., and Richard E. Porter, eds. *Intercultural Communication: A Reader.* Belmont, Calif.: Wadsworth, 1991.

Stewart, Edward C., and Milton J. Bennett. *American Cultural Patterns: A Cross-Cultural Perspective.* Yarmouth, Maine: Intercultural Press, 1991.

Publishers/Organizations

Intercultural Press, Inc., P.O. Box 700, Yarmouth, Maine 04096 (publishes books on a wide variety of cross-cultural topics) (207–846–5168)

SIETAR International (Society for Intercultural Education, Training, and Research), 733 15th St., N.W., Suite 900, Washington, D.C. 20005 (202–737–5000)

About the Authors

Deena Levine, M.A., has been a consultant in cross-cultural communication for over ten years, having built her career on her earlier work in the TEFL/TESL (Teaching English as a Foreign/Second Language) field. She conducts workshops, seminars, and courses in cross-cultural awareness and skills for teachers, social service providers, and businesspeople. Ms. Levine has also co-authored a second ESL/EFL text: *The Culture Puzzle: Cross-Cultural Communication for English as a Second Language* (1987). She is currently working on a book dealing with the challenges of managing multicultural law enforcement.

Mara Adelman, Ph.D., is an assistant professor in the Department of Communication Studies at Northwestern University in Chicago. Her primary research interests are in the use of social support systems in coping with stress and adapting to change. She is co-author of the book *Communicating Social Support* (1987). Her review on social support and adaptation was published in the *International Journal for Intercultural Relations* (1988). Ms. Adelman was awarded an Interculturalist Award by the Society for Intercultural Education, Training, and Research for her contribution to this field.